Amazing Secrets of
NEW AVATAR POWER

Amazing Secrets of NEW AVATAR POWER

Geof Gray-Cobb

Re-edited by VcToria Gray,
daughter of Geof Gray-Cobb

Amazing Secrets of New Avatar Power
© 1978 by Geof Gray-Cobb

ISBN 978-1-9991283-2-6

Revised Edition, January 2020

All rights reserved. No part of this book may be reproduced in any form or by any means, without permission in writing from the publisher.

This book is a reference work based on research by the author.

The Alternative Universe Alberta, Canada

Geof Gray-Cobb's Dedication from the original book

To all my readers, both old and new, without whose encouragement and intelligent questioning I might never have seen the need to improve that which went before. Herewith my latest offering: may it help you to reach all your goals.

VcToria's Dedication

I am dedicating this book to the unseen. The helpers, Angels, spirit guides and all of the Universal energy that has helped me take gigantic strides in my life. Without the signs and actions, my life would have little purpose. May the Universe keep sending me the peace I have learnt to attain.

May this book, and all the one's I have re-published help you, the reader, to whom I also dedicate the blessed energy that you can create as I have done.

Other books by Geof Gray-Cobb
(AKA Frater Malak)

The Mystic Grimoire of Mighty Spells and Rituals – Here are the most superior Spells and powerful Rituals—the bare bones of magic—set down step-by-step in plain, clear English by Frater Malak. Re-published in April 2019.
ISBN: 978-0-9812138-5-9

NAP: The Miracle of New Avatar Power – How the secrets of the ancients are able to bring to you the life you are looking for. Follow Geof Gray-Cobb and the knowledge he imparts to you from years of research. Re-published in May 2019.
ISBN: 978-0-9812138-7-3

Helping Yourself with Acupineology – Through the simple and painless techniques of stimulating the mystic pineal section of the brain, you can direct the energy field that flows around your body to draw to you happiness, health, freedom and money, easily and automatically. Originally revealed and published by Geof Gray-Cobb in 1980. Re-published in July 2019.
ISBN: 978-1-9991283-0-2

Secrets From Beyond the Pyramids – Based on his understanding of the awesome power of the Pyramids, Geof Gray-Cobb shows you how New Psychic Energy Power can quickly and easily transform your present existence into a life of deep and lasting satisfaction. Re-published in November 2019.
ISBN: 978-1-9991283-1-9

The Encyclopedia of Fifty-Year-Old Magic by Frater Malak, Geof Gray-Cobb, Maiya Gray-Cobb and VcToria Gray-Cobb. This is the only book you will ever need to change your life with magic, positive energy and learning to let go of whatever holds you back. Taken from the collec-tive works of Frater Malak [AKA Geof Gray-Cobb], Geof Gray-Cobb and Maiya Gray-Cobb, the BEST of the BEST will be re-published. Their daughter, VcToria Gray-Cobb, will add her own take on what you can shift. This book will show you who YOUR Angels are and who you can use to guide you to the success of YOUR own life. It will let you know what Moon sign to work under with the spells and rituals and will bring you the POWER of ALL. To be released by December 2020.
ISBN: 978-1-9991283-5-7

All books are available in eBook format.

WHAT THIS BOOK CAN DO FOR YOU

You simply have to name it. Literally! This whole book could be taken up with telling you about the fantastic things you can achieve with its help.

Health. Wealth. Happiness. They're just words until you actually experience them. And you shall. A cascade of cash and goods to fill your every need. Those, too. Commanding the minds of your colleagues. No problem. Canceling evil conditions as if they had never existed. Simple! Making your loved ones ecstatic with your habits and restored virility. Easy. Gaining raises and promotions. Bringing business to you. Helping your doctor banish sickness so that you glow with youthful vigor and health. All those, and more………more………more……….

PERSONAL MIRACLES ARE YOURS

Sure, I could go on. I could quote you letter after letter from grateful people who have turned their lives from misery to ecstasy and triumph by applying the suggestions I'm going to give you. Some of these can come later, as examples of what can be done.

But let's not waste time here in giving a great many examples—you want these splendid things to happen to *you*, not to someone else, isn't that right?

What I'm offering you is a way to change your life to whatever you wish it to be, without major physical efforts, without long hours of concentrated study—without anything more than applying *Amazing Secrets of New Avatar Power* which are spelled out for you in the following pages.

VcToria Comments: As I have mentioned in the four previous books I have re-published, I have taken out all of the testimonials from letters that Dad received. This has made the book more manageable to get to the heart of the practice. It has also lowered his original books considerable in cost.

WHAT IS NEW AVATAR POWER?

Let's get that behind us early on. *New Avatar Power* is a name. Nothing more: It's a name for a sparkling, miracle-working natural energy which everyone has around him.

Your mind, body, and soul run on *New Avatar Power*, and so does the whole Universe: the planets circle on their appointed orbits, the earth revolves, the

WHAT THIS BOOK CAN DO FOR YOU

wind blows, and you exist within an ocean of this natural energy.

This energy is not new. The ancients knew it, possibly better than we do today. Many sects, secret societies, cults, and metaphysical teachers are aware of this energy and advise how to make best use of it.

What I am offering to you is not an undiscovered power to which I lay claim as the discoverer or inventor. My position in the equation is to offer you a valid way of *employing* the energy, explaining to you in detail, simply, how you can latch on to the currents in this tide of energy and use it to shape your entire existence.

The name *New Avatar Power* comes from a previous book of mine, *The Miracle of New Avatar Power*. This book is, if you will, an extension of that first book. Earlier readers will recognize some of the techniques I'm going to describe, and if you read the dedication at the beginning of this volume, you'll see why it had to be written.

But to dispel any misconceptions, although the *method* is mine, the Power is Universal, and is called Godpower by some, Christ Consciousness by others, Eloptic Energy, Psychic Power, Animal Magnetism...the list has been almost endless, and lengthens daily. But the energy we're talking about is the Unseen Ocean of Life-Force which blends the Universe into a harmonious whole.

With that point established, we can proceed. You may, for instance, be thinking, *"New Avatar Power?* I've read about it. So I don't need this book."

Wait one minute, if you please: This book is truly *new*. In the past four years I've read a small mountain of mail, accepted suggestions, analyzed the failures (I'll tell you about those soon), and personally worked with this fresh approach to *New Avatar Power* to refine the method, to make it even simpler, and to make it more efficient.

WHAT THIS BOOK CAN DO FOR YOU

Have I succeeded? Very much so! As I said in my previous book, the following is not intended as an outing for my ego, nor is it intended to make you envious. I merely state what follows to show you that I've *used New Avatar Power*, made it work for me, and I'm not just mouthing theories while I starve in a garret.

On page 12 of *The Miracle of New Avatar Power* I illustrated *New Avatar Power* in action. I mentioned a five-figure bank balance, a rare and expensive sports-car, a luxurious penthouse in eastern Canada, and the success pattern which *New Avatar Power* had enabled me to reach from not very encouraging beginnings.

VcToria Comments: This reference would be on page xiii in the republished version of *The Miracle of New Avatar Power*, May 2019.

While preparing the basic work for *this* book, and experimenting with the methods to get maximum effects, *New Avatar Power* has taken me higher, even more harmoniously and happily.

The penthouse is in the past. The racing car is still going strong, with a second car added for convenience. Now Maiya; my wife, and I own a ranch in the country. I'm typing this manuscript at a desk looking out over our land, across our creek at a mighty river and snow-capped mountains on the edge of the West Canadian wilderness, yet close enough to civilization to get out and get involved when we feel so inclined.

A small continuation of an episode I mentioned in *The Miracle New Avatar Power* may interest you. Remember on page 13, I. described how, after getting into *New Avatar Power* use, my bald spot grew hair again, amazing my barber?

VcToria Comments: Again these words above are on page xiii of the republished book: May 2019.

WHAT THIS BOOK CAN DO FOR YOU

That was over four years ago, and I'm no youngster. My beard has grown gray and grizzled (Maiya says she likes it that way, so I must not *New Avatar Power* it any other color!). But my hair's growing like I was 18 again: every month I walk out of my barber's looking like a bank clerk of 20 years ago, and within four weeks I go back in looking like a hippie who never knew what scissors were for! And Maiya keeps asking when I'm going to grow gray and distinguished! No dyes, no treatment—just dark, dark hair keeps growing.

A small point, indeed, but illustrating that, as I constantly repeat, *anything* is possible with *New Avatar Power*.

Yes, it continues to work for me. Many of you will have seen me enjoying myself on a TV panel game from Canada, called "Beyond Reason" and doing an astrological spot on a talk show. On average, I now spend about ten days each month working—if that's what you call doing what you enjoy most—and the rest of the month I do anything Maiya and I fancy.

Please don't feel jealous as I tell you what a ball life is for me. I know that's the glad results of applying *New Avatar Power*. You can do it, too. In fact, you're the *only* person who can use *New Avatar Power* to satisfactorily change your life, so don't you go laying out any of your hard-earned cash to anyone who says they'll change your life *for* you. *New Avatar Power* works differently—and you've got the method right here. You need no other assistance.

Yes, you *can* use *New Avatar Power* to be and do what you wish. I know: I've got the letters here to prove my case is no fluke.

VcToria Comments: As previously mentioned, I have removed the testimonials in the re-edited and re-published books. HOWEVER! I have chosen to leave the

WHAT THIS BOOK CAN DO FOR YOU

first one in as the following paragraph talks about those who send letters with 'IT DOESN'T WORK"

NEW AVATAR POWER HAS HELPED THOUSANDS

Four years of reading delighted success letters, four years of mail by the sackful has shown me that I'm not wandering in cloud cuckoo land when I extol the virtues of *New Avatar Power.*

Literally thousands of people just like yourself have discovered *New Avatar Power* and found freedom from want, new health, and glorious happiness. Even the most skeptical and unbelieving have been forced to admit, "I didn't believe it could happen to me" as they've seen their lives transformed.

Maybe it's time for just one example from the many, sufficing to illustrate what I mean. And this is by no means a special case: I have used this pair of letters taken at random from hundreds like them.

His Hopeless Life Changed
to Progress and Contentment!

Let Neil J. of Texas tell his own story, in his own words. Following are actual extracts from two letters he sent me just six months apart. We could almost wonder if they both were written by the same person. I assure you they were.

Here is the significant body of Neil's first letter, written shakily on scraps of paper from a notebook.

"I bought your book, and I am writing to you in desperation. My doctor says I am beyond hope. My dear wife died earlier this year. So did my beloved brother. I am alone. After 15 years, I have been told by my employer that they can no longer use me. I am ashamed to say I am on the way to Skid Row. Last night is an alcoholic blank. I woke up this morning in a drunk tank. I

WHAT THIS BOOK CAN DO FOR YOU

stink. I am sick. I am not even brave enough to end it all.

"I opened it at a money ritual and called for money. Nothing happened, as I expected it wouldn't. The smells of drains and the filth didn't go away. My blanket and clothes continued to stink of vomit. No one knocked on the door and gave me the bag of gold I asked for. I am still in this third floor walk-up rooming house filled with derelicts as I soon shall be.

"Your book doesn't work. I knew it wouldn't. I was a fool to buy it when I could have used the money for food, or a bottle of wine. Thought you would like to hear from a loser for a change while I still have the wits and strength to write."

I wrote a brief note, suggesting Neil should apply the *whole* book, not just dip into it, and I added thoughts about other points he might attend to. I honestly figured I'd never hear from him again,

Surprise! Almost six months to the day from his first bitter and despairing letter, here's what I received from him, written in a firm hand on the expensive business paper of a financial advisory organization. Not until I'd read it through did I notice Neil's name printed up top: he had become an executive director,

"If you calculate I invested less than 10 dollars in your book the investment has paid off 10,000-fold in half a year in cold, hard cash, not counting any side benefits or invested assets. That's a yearly gain of one-million percentum, if you're interested in the figures.

"I did as you said: followed your book. It worked, and I'm not fabricating: this business depends totally on truth and accuracy.

"Where to begin? So much has happened. I got your letter, and even bemused and sodden as I was at that time (seems centuries ago) I realized you made sense. Picking five lines almost at random out of your book was like trying to bake a loaf without flour.

"Things started happening. Too many to waste your valuable time listing in detail: got a job, was promoted, teamed up with a new friend, started this service organization. It boomed. I *own* a 12-room split-level, a Cadillac, my own private Lear jet. From a near alcoholic loser I've zoomed up to be a pillar of the community.

"Perfect? Well, I'm still working with *New Avatar Power* to try to cut back on my 30-hour working week to give me more leisure to explore, but meantime I have a wedding to attend. Mine! And *she's* perfect. I thought my first marriage was tremendous, but this one promises to be 100 times better. My doctor says he doesn't know why I got well: he once gave me 6 months. Now he's given me 60 *years*.

"P.S. Pardon my writing this in longhand. I could have had one of my three secretaries write to you but I'm afraid if one of them finds out about *New Avatar Power*, she might take my job!"

"IT DOESN'T WORK"

Face it: as well as letters like Neil's, I get letters from failures, and despite my advice, follow up letters suggested they continued to fail to find the magic within *New Avatar Power* to make life go better.

That worried me. I used to ask myself where I'd gone wrong. *New Avatar Power* is a universal energy, and *everyone* should be able to use it.

I kept the "Don't Work" letters in a separate pile. Not a large pile, but large enough to be a burr under my saddle. About one person in every 200 insisted they'd seen nothing happen to them at all when they tried to use *New Avatar Power*.

Some were simple to fathom. Like Neil when he started, they'd pulled a few words off a page, ignored

WHAT THIS BOOK CAN DO FOR YOU

how to use those words, and promptly written me a despairing letter.

Agreed, you can chant until you're red in the face and nothing in happen, unless you add the necessary extra simple ingredients. And they *are* simple, but vital. I'll be telling you about them as we go along.

Yet a hard core of failures assured me they'd followed my instructions right down the line, and "it still didn't work."

That took some research to solve, especially as the clue was staring me in the face. But solve it I did, discovering the *Secret of Mysterious* N'T *Words* which can divert *New Avatar Power* and sadly slow its ability to help you to happiness. Very powerful words they are too, and while they have definite use in this world, identifying them was a major step toward turning the dismal failures to glorious succeeders. That *Secret* is in Chapter 3 of this book and has never, to my knowledge, appeared in print before.

With that powerful weapon for preventing the inhibition of *New Avatar Power* discovered, one other obstacle came to light which was consistently preventing the "Don't Work's" from achieving their promised happiness, harmony, and wealth. Overcoming the obstacle requires nothing absolutely new: it forms part of the original *Miracle of New Avatar Power* method. But in this book I've exposed it a bit more clearly, emphasized it, because it's the kernel of the nut of using your psychic powers for personal gain and success.

Follow through here, and *this* time the "Don't Work's" will be one in a thousand...even less. I *know* this method works. Prove with me. What have you got to lose, except your debts, misery, and pain? Replace them with wealth, happiness, and well-being, easily, naturally, and automatically with the *Secrets of New Avatar Power*.

WHAT THIS BOOK CAN DO FOR YOU

VcToria Comments: No more 'letters' will be published in this newly edited book. All the wording for the shifts to be created will remain the same.

Now that the cost of the original book has fallen, if you wish to buy it to read all the 'letters' that were published please feel free to do so. They are available with second hand book stores. I do not sell them.

THIS BOOK IS SELF-CONTAINED

Lest you've gained the impression that to make *New Avatar Power* work you need to have read my previous book, I hasten to reassure you.

If you've read *The Miracle of New Avatar Power*, all well and good. Add these tips, modify your working with *New Avatar Power* for greater simplicity, and thus improve your success score.

No need to worry if you've never even *heard* of *The Miracle of New Avatar Power* before. This book says it all for you, in careful detail.

Step by step I explain just what you need to do to achieve your deepest desires and fondest wishes. Each amazing *Secret* and its ancillary work is summarized at the end of each chapter, so you can review how far you've come as you finish reading and applying each *Secret*.

All I ask of you is that you read *all* of this book, accepting the leadings I offer. The chapter summaries are merely to remind you of what you have just read: trying to use the summaries because you're impatient to see and experience your personal miracles will merely slow things down for you.

So, no dipping! Follow through on this, one step at a time. Then instead of *reading* about these incredible miracles, you'll find them happening to you—in sudden bursts of good fortune which will turn your friends green with envy and have your enemies gnashing their teeth in frustration.

AMAZING SECRETS ARE BETTER, SIMPLER, AND EVEN MORE EFFECTIVE

A car? It's yours. A new home? *Secrets of New Avatar Power* will bring it to you. A loving partner? Simple, and with the added bonus that he or she can be far more harmonious for you than anyone you *think* is for you. Wealth? Add up how much you really need, and you've got it. Enemies hurting you? Smash! They're helpless to disturb you. Disappointed in your achievements? Decide what's right for you, what you'd like to do, where you'd like to go and destiny bears it to you, on a golden platter.

Unrecognized at work or in the community? So aim for status, reputation, position—and up you go. Health not responding to medical help? *Amazing Secrets* will tune your body and mind to bring you back to bubbling well-being.

And it's all so self-generating, easy, and quicker than you'd dared to hope.

All those things—and anything else I may have missed—are yours for the taking. To enjoy. To savor. To indulge in. To make the harmonious, happy person you deserve to be.

Never let anyone sell you the false bill of goods that you do not deserve happiness. That's the way the Universe was planned. And you're swimming in a sea of *New Avatar Power* which will, when directed, do your bidding. *The Amazing Secrets* merely explain how to make *Your Avatar Power* work—because if you're not happy, obviously your inner powers need stirring up and aligning.

And the way to stir them up is right here.

Yes, *The Miracle of New Avatar Power* was good. Now, developed from my exchanges with readers, the *Amazing Secrets* are better. Better because they're *simpler* than almost all other methods of tapping your inner energies. Better because they're *more effective* than previous techniques.

What you now hold in your hands is a refinement of an already excellent method. *Gone are many of the special words which caused some people to stumble, thinking the way you said them* was vital to success. That's a fallacy, but it was nevertheless an imagined obstacle. So out they go.

Added are the specific 21 *Secrets* which, applied to your life, bring true harmony with Natural Law, with consequent growth and meaningful progress.

And, of all people, I should like to sincerely thank the "Don't Works." If it hadn't been for your sad letters, I might never have been prompted to refine and expand this method of applying *New Avatar Power*.

WHAT TO EXPECT FROM THESE AMAZING SECRETS

Turn these pages, absorb the words. Apply the suggestions and you're on your way to a peak of satisfaction you may have thought was reserved for special people. A peak of *freedom*: freedom to work if you wish, play when you wish, to laze around, if that's what you want. To be *yourself*, to come and go as you please with a joy of living which is beyond the reach of many.

In a way that peak *is* for special people: and you're one of them—once you've awakened your automatic destiny changer: *New Avatar Power*.

WHAT THIS BOOK CAN DO FOR YOU

APPLYING NEW AVATAR POWER SECRETS IS SIMPLE

When using *New Avatar Power Secrets*, do you have to fast for a week? Make wild signs and gestures? Moan, groan, wail, chant, roar, and invoke Unknown Words of Power? Give up smoking, drinking, sex, or other normal habits? Collect a closetful of weird trinkets, amulets, wands, and assorted arcane objects? Strip to the buff or wear sackcloth robes?

Well, now, if you feel it will help you, you're most welcome to do any of the above. *But none are necessary.* Most are undesirable, in fact. Yes, I will ask you to wave your arms about gently in the privacy of your room, if convenient. You'll be saying *some* Words of Power—but there's little that's mysterious about them. Your *Confidential Corporeal Commands* and *Personal Verbal Seals* are part of the *Secrets*, and you construct them a step at a time, understanding exactly what you're saying.

That removes yet another worry for some, who feel when they call on a Mystic Being whose name they don't recognize, they may be calling down Dark Powers or something equally spooky.

Applying *New Avatar Power Secrets* is truly simple. Most of you work with them without anyone else knowing you're doing it. They might wonder why you get all the luck, but unless you tell, no one will learn that you're changing your life with the awesome energy of *New Avatar Power*.

THE FOUR DOORS TO THE AMAZING SECRETS OF NEW AVATAR POWER

Your mind works well with pictures: that's why instruction books often carry many illustrations. When working with *New Avatar Power* you are channeling it

WHAT THIS BOOK CAN DO FOR YOU

through your mind. So a useful way of opening up to *New Avatar Power* is to use your imagination.

What I suggest you do is to pretend you're opening doors to treasure chambers. Of course, you're not opening any actual, physical doors—these are names we apply to the states you pass through as you apply the *Secrets*.

Look at it this way. If you're not yet using your *New Avatar Power*, we can liken you to someone who is locked outside a castle in a storm. If you think of fate as the storm, you're blown every which way, soaked and chilled by the rain, scared by thunder, hurt by lightning and falling tree branches, perhaps attacked by wolves.

Few such things happen to us in this day and age, but if you think of credit collectors as wolves, sudden changes in your working life as lightning, home or industrial accidents as falling tree branches, and similar comparisons, you'll realize how we can compare your harassed life to this lone traveler cowering in the downpour outside the castle where he knows safety and warmth exist within.

Yes, you *can* leave your troubles in the past and change to the luxury, riches, and happiness which are your birthright, and that change in lifestyle can be likened to leaving a stormy, perilous place and taking shelter in a warm and protective environment.

How to get inside? To continue our metaphor, you pass first through the *Iron Door* in the outer wall.

This simulates your first step toward using *New Avatar Power Secrets*. *Opening the Iron Door* is a step which also involves what I have named your *Mystic Initiation*. The very next chapter tells you all about finding the key to the *Iron Door*, swinging it open, and learning the *First New Avatar Power Secret*.

Continuing this idea of your being a traveler, you're now sheltered from the storm by the castle walls, but you've only reached the courtyard. The wind is less violent, but you're still unprotected from the rain and thunder.

So you move next to the *Bronze Door,* and as you find out how to open it with a simple mind technique, you learn your *Confidential Corporeal Commands* and acquire the *Second* and *Third New Avatar Power Secrets.*

Warmer now, but still dripping wet (if you keep the picture I'm expressing in mind), you're faced with the *Silver Door.*

Special passwords get you inside, and as you learn the *Fifth* to *Seventh Secrets,* you also discover the *Mysterious* N'T *Words.*

You're now facing the fourth and final *Golden Door.* Inside is food, a crackling fire, dry clothing—everything which symbolizes the best in life. Once you're inside, you can cast off everything which is holding you back or making you miserable. Your *Personal Verbal Seals* will gain you entry through the Golden Door, behind which lies the vital *Eighth New Avatar Power Secret.*

Here you tie together everything you've done so far, and follow by being shown the *Ninth* through *Twenty-First Secrets.*

Weary traveler, you have arrived. Your personal miracles await your command. Identify your need, and see *New Avatar Power* swing into action. Read on, and join me on this fascinating journey, to control an energy which makes *anything* possible for you.

Geof Gray-Cobb

Table of Contents

WHAT THIS BOOK CAN DO FOR YOU 1
   Personal Miracles Are Yours 2
   What Is New Avatar Power? 2
   New Avatar Power Has Helped Thousands 6
      His Hopeless Life Changed to Progress and Contentment! 6
   "It Doesn't Work" 8
   This Book Is Self-Contained 10
   Amazing Secrets Are Better, Simpler, And Even More Effective 11
   What To Expect From These Amazing Secrets 12
   Applying New Avatar Power Secrets Is Simple 13
   The Four Doors To The Amazing Secrets Of New Avatar Power 13

1. ENTERING THE IRON DOOR: YOUR MYSTIC INITIATION TO NEW AVATAR POWER 25
   New Avatar Power Is All Around You 28
   How To Believe In The Reality Of Cosmic Energy 29
   How To Hear Cosmic Energy 30
   How To See Cosmic Energy 32
   Now You Are Convinced It Exists, Cosmic Energy Can Be Directed By Your Own Mind Vitality 34
   Cosmic Energy Is The Most Powerful Force In The Universe 34
   New Avatar Power Is Holy And Pure 35
   New Avatar Power Welcomes An Aiming Point 36
   First Secret Of New Avatar Power 37

CONTENTS

Change Is The Key To Using New Avatar Power 38
What Needs Changing In Your Life? 38
Your Mystic Initiation 38
Onward, Through The Bronze Door 41
Summary Of Chapter 1 42

2. INSIDE THE BRONZE DOOR: YOUR CONFIDENTIAL CORPOREAL AVATAR COMMANDS 45

Physical Tension May Impede New Avatar Power 48
How To Banish Conditions Which Slow Down Your New Avatar Power 49
Your Confidential Corporeal Commands 49
When To Use Your Confidential Corporeal Commands 52
Important First New Avatar Power Steps 53
Signs That Your Condfidential Corporeal Commands Are Working 54
Start Making Life Easier With Your Confidential Corporeal Commands 55
Second Secret Of New Avatar Power: The Fabulous Fear Eradicator 56
Third Secret Of New Avatar Power: The Extraordinary Happiness Restorer 59
Summary Of Chapter 2 60

3. BEHIND THE SILVER DOOR: THE WONDERS OF MYSTERIOUS AVATAR POWER WORDS 63

Thoughts And Words Can Be Impeding Vibrations .. 66
Fourth Secret Of New Avatar Power: The Mysterious "N'T" Words 66
How To Banish The Mysterious N'T Words 68

CONTENTS

Playing The Mysterious N'T Word Game 69

Fifth Secret Of New Avatar Power: The Superb Uncertainty Banisher... 71

Sixth Secret Of New Avatar Power: The Unique Creativity Regenerator 73

Seventh Secret Of New Avatar Power: Defending Yourself With New Avatar Power 75

New Avatar Power Leads Unerringly To A New Superlative Way Of Life For you 76

Early Signs That New Avatar Power Is Doing Its Marvelous Work.. 78

Summary Of Chapter 3... 79

4. BEYOND THE GOLDEN DOOR: YOUR PERSONAL AVATAR VERBAL SEALS.. 81

What Your Personal Verbal Seals Can Do For You.. 84

Decide On Your Admiration Targets 85

Eighth Secret Of New Avatar Power: Creating Your Personal Verbal Seals 87

How To Use Your Personal Verbal Seals 89

Everything You've Learned So Far Knits Into A Perfect Life-Changing Package.. 90

You'll Be Amazed To Compare Your Future With Your Past... 91

Summary Of Chapter 4... 92

5. STEP BY STEP MIRACLES FOR YOU 95

Let New Avatar Power Do The Work 98

Ninth Secret Of The New Avatar Power: The Incredible Disinterest Remover 98

Tenth Secret Of New Avatar Power: The Stupendous Power Enricher 100

CONTENTS

The Seven Negative Traps 101
The Seven Desirable States 102
Your Mental Achievement Chalkboard 103
Summary Of Chapter 5 104

6. SPECIAL WAYS TO USE THE SECRETS OF NEW AVATAR POWER 107

Some Situations Need The Strongest New Avatar Power Techniques 110
Fate Sets Up Part Of Your Future For You To Work Through 110
Eleventh Secret Of New Avatar Power: The Fantastic Loneliness Eliminator 111
Twelfth Secret Of New Avatar Power: The Startling Astral Travel Inducer 113
Best Times And Conditions For Astral Travel 116
Get Ahead By Knowing What's Going To Happen .. 118
Thirteenth Secret Of New Avatar Power: The Magic Future-Knowing Technique 119
Freewill Is Of Great Importance 121
Summary Of Chapter 6 122

7. SECRETS OF TOTAL HAPPINESS THROUGH NEW AVATAR POWER TECHNIQUES 125

Your Total Happiness List 129
Fourteenth Secret Of New Avatar Power: The Miraculous Despair Deflector 130
Banish Bad And Replace It With Good 133
Fifteenth Secret Of New Avatar Power: The Spontaneous Health Regenerator 133
Reshaping Your Dreams To Bring Benefits 136
How To Invade The Sleeping Minds Of Others 137

CONTENTS

- Sixteenth Secret Of New Avatar Power: Charging Your Aura With Cosmic Energy 138
- What A Charged Aura Can Do To Your Colleagues 140
- Summary Of Chapter 7 141

8. SECRETS OF WEALTH—INCREDIBLE NEW AVATAR MONEY ACTIVATORS 143

- Where All The Money Is 146
- Why You Probably Have Less Than Your Rightful Share 147
- How To Acquire Money And Property 147
- Seventeenth Secret Of New Avatar Power: The Phenomenal Over-Sensitivity Transformer 148
- Eighteenth Secret Of New Avatar Power: The Remarkable Money Renewer 150
- Where Will The Money Come From? 153
- How To Maintain Your Bank Balance Once It's Healthy 153
- Summary Of Chapter 8 155

9. SECRETS OF PERFECT LOVE, ROMANCE AND MARRIAGE: HOW NEW AVATAR POWER BRINGS YOU THE LOVE YOU DESERVE 157

- You Deserve Love And Romance: New Avatar Power Will Bring It 160
- Aim High With New Avatar Power 160
- Nineteenth Secret Of New Avatar Power: The Exceptional Love Elevator 161
- Making The Most Effective Use Of The Exceptional Love Elevator 162
- Age Or Appearance Is Unimportant 164
- An Arcane Truth About Marriage Bonds 165

CONTENTS

    The Choice Is Yours 165
    Summary Of Chapter 9 166

10. SECRETS OF GOOD FORTUNE THROUGH AMAZING NEW AVATAR POWER 169

    What's Your Idea Of Good Luck? 172
    How Luck Works 173
    How To Help Lady Luck Smile On You 174
    Twentieth Secret Of New Avatar Power: The Marvelous Luck Changer 174
    How To Use The Marvelous Luck Changer 176
    Discovering Winning Numbers 177
    Summary Of Chapter 10 178

11. SECRETS OF ESCAPING FROM DOMINATION USING NEW AVATAR POWER 181

    How to Recognize The Domination Which Is Crippling You 183
    Escaping From Domination 185
    Twenty-First Secret Of New Avatar Power: The Wonderful Over-Concern Protector 186
    Defeating Your Enemies 187
    Removing Curses, The Evil Eye Or Possession 187
    Summary Of Chapter 11 189

12. CREATING YOUR PERFECT LIFE WITH NEW AVATAR POWER 191

    Best Ways To Apply The Whole New Avatar Power Technique 194
    Details To Watch 194
    Follow The Instructions And Your Miracles Arrive. 196
    Daily New Avatar Power Workout Is Best 196

CONTENTS

Total Attunement Using New Avatar Power 197
EPILOG: SOME PERSONAL THOUGHTS TO YOU FROM THE AUTHOR IN 1978 201
New Avatar Power Is Waiting To Serve You 205
EPILOG FROM VcToria 206

Amazing Secrets of
NEW AVATAR POWER

Entering The Iron Door: Your Mystic Initiation To New Avatar Power

1

ENTERING THE IRON DOOR: YOUR MYSTIC INITIATION TO NEW AVATAR POWER

You're on your way, about to take an early step toward "tuning yourself in" to the life-changing and life-maintaining energy around you.

For the very best results with this book, I suggest you first read through to the end. Try not to skip over any parts, because it's often a feature of instructions such as these that a single line of the most unlikely

INITIATION TO NEW AVATAR POWER

piece of narrative may contain exactly the piece of information you need to firmly latch onto the method.
Every line of this narrative has been included with good reason. No padding fills these pages: everything is designed to show you how to put your *New Avatar Power* into glorious and fulfilling action.

Note: As you read, you'll come across suggestions which tell you not to proceed to the next chapter until you've mastered the previous one. Those suggestions apply only when you begin to work with and use this method of life-changing with *New Avatar Power*. The instructions are *not* intended to prevent your reading this book through to the end to find out what it's about.

NEW AVATAR POWER IS ALL AROUND YOU

Have you ever watched a plant growing? It grows quietly, without fuss; the seed swells and pushes out a rootlet. A tiny seedling thrusts up through the soil, and as time passes the seedling becomes a leaf on a stem, grows branches, flowers, fruits, or does whatever nature intended that plant to do.

That seed is using Cosmic Energy to grow. It's attuned to the Laws of Nature, and it just grows. Allow a bean to sprout, then deliberately plant it upside down, with the root uppermost and the leaf down. Within days the bean will have aligned itself with Cosmic Energy to put things right. The root curls over and grows down, while the leaf twists around and reaches for the light.

That, in a very real sense, is what you're going to do with your *New Avatar Power Secrets*. You're going to use it to put things *right* in your life, to bring growth and fulfillment.

You're immersed in the same ocean of Cosmic Energy as the bean is, and your body, mind, and soul can use it to grow.

INITIATION TO NEW AVATAR POWER

If you're unhappy, disturbed, unpeaceful, and at odds with the world, you could think of yourself as being like that bean planted upside down. *You're not in tune with Cosmic Energy.*

Circumstances, environment, and not knowing precisely what to do for the best, are preventing you from putting your life to rights. Your root is pointing upward, and your leaf is seeking daylight deeper in the earth—if you don't mind being compared to an upside down bean!

That's exactly where *New Avatar Power Secrets* come in. By applying them, you automatically put yourself in phase, in tune, with Cosmic Energy, and your life becomes as carefree, progressive, and ongoing as that little bean plant.

HOW TO BELIEVE IN THE REALITY OF COSMIC ENERGY

You've read my preceding words, understood the idea of the bean plant growing, perhaps even accepted the concept of your being able to tune yourself to Cosmic Energy and Natural Law by using *New Avatar Power Secrets*.

Yet perhaps a small doubt niggles. Pardon my pun, but you're not an ordinary bean—you're a *human* bean! Is there *really* an unseen energy which can make your life as productive and up thrusting as a healthy plant?

To banish such doubts is simple. What if you could *hear* this energy, even *see* it, with your own eyes and ears? Then even the strongest doubt, at the deepest levels of your mind, that this energy is not a reality would be removed.

INITIATION TO NEW AVATAR POWER

HOW TO HEAR COSMIC ENERGY

Somewhere in your daily routines or in the still of the night, you can find a quiet place. Perhaps life is a constant racket of Musak, TV, machines, traffic, trains, kids, and city hubbub. Somehow, somewhere, some when, in order to *hear* Cosmic Energy, you must find an island of quiet.

You need only about two minutes of silence, so you're not seeking a total impossibility. If necessary go out to find silence. An empty church, the far hills or deep woods, the basement of an office building—anywhere remote from the cacophony which forms a background to our routines so much these days.

It's worth arranging a special excursion, alone, to seek this silent time.

Now, if it's truly hand-on-heart, I-tried-and-failed *impossible* for you to find a quiet place, disregard this step. But please do not take the easy way out: I urge you to *try* to make it. You need to do this only once, and the benefits to your mental patterns and subsequent success with *New Avatar Power* are incalculable.

This chapter refers to your *Mystic Initiation*. Hearing Cosmic Energy is a part of it.

I'll assume you've found your quiet place. Read on carefully, because describing *sounds* is a challenge, words being blunt tools to capture the Cosmic Music you're going to hear. And lest you be misled by my use of the word "music," this is nothing like the sounds the Boston Pops or the Rolling Stones make! I say *music* because you're listening to the harmony of the Universe.

At last it's silent around you. Proceed as follows. Cup both your hands and cover your ears, fingers slightly curved and pointing toward the top of your head, elbows down and to the front. Just a natural relaxed position, and it's unimportant whether you're

30

standing, sitting, kneeling or lying down, provided you can put your hands over your ears.

Gently, with only sufficient pressure for you to feel the heels of your hands against your jaw is correct. Yes, left hand on left ear, right hand on right ear—I promised the use of *New Avatar Power Secrets* would not place you in any difficult contortions, and I meant it.

Turn your sharpest attention to what you're hearing. The low-pitched throb, rumble, or flutter is your heart pumping blood around your head. Listen to it: the inner workings of your physical body. But *do not strain too hard to hear it*: you're most certainly listening to *something*, so memorize that noise, however it sounds to you.

Now move your palms a fraction at a time away from your ears. Either move your hands away from your head, very slowly, or use the heels of your hands against your jaw as pivots to swing your fingers away from your ears. Uncover: but dead, *dead* slow.

When your palms are about an inch from your ears, notice how the noise you're hearing has changed. The "dullness" leaves, and a kind of *high-pitched hiss*, almost a whistle, replaces the louder sounds you heard with your hands close to your head.

The nearest I can describe this "hiss" is that it sounds like an auto tire quietly going down, perhaps with almost imperceptible musical undertones—like a military parade several miles away.

Experiment with this. Repeat the ears-covered-palms-slowly-removed routine. Compare the sounds you hear. Maybe you get lucky the very first time, and distinctly hear the musical hiss I've battled to describe to you. On the other hand it may take several attempts before you hear what I'm indicating.

That steady hiss is Cosmic Energy being detected by your body and mind. Some people who listen to it say the faint "music" I referred to comes through quite clearly after a while.

If you can hear this sound of star-creating Cosmic Energy, you're a step ahead: your logical, conscious mind is being given audible and undeniable evidence that Cosmic Energy is a reality, not wishful thinking or imagination.

What if you fail to hear this energy flow? Worry not—some people indeed cannot detect it, most often because they're not sure what they're listening for. It's faint, but definite, but if you do not pick it up, there's no need to go up the wall. Skip this step and go on to the next. But *give it a try* before you abandon it: leaving out suggested steps in this process of using *New Avatar Power* is merely inviting slower progress.

HOW TO SEE COSMIC ENERGY

Seeing is believing, they say. And here we're going to *show* you Cosmic Energy. Once you've seen it, no logical argument will ever be able to convince you of its non-existence.

No special environment needed for this simple technique. Merely reasonable bright lighting conditions. Normal daylight coming through a window is perfect. A desk light, a ceiling fixture, a fluorescent tube—any source of light bright enough to read by is your aim.

Warning: Do **not** use the direct disc of the sun as your light source. That can blind you.

Hold up the hand you normally write with. Ambidextrous people have a choice! Put your thumb and forefinger together just as you would to pick up a pencil or similar small object. Touch them lightly together, and move your hand until you see your fingers silhouetted against the light. Within reason, the brighter the light source, the better—but if it's so bright it makes you squint, or your eyes water, it's too bright.

Look closely where your finger and thumb are touching. Move them apart as slowly as you can. Close one eye, or put your free hand over one eye, and focus clearly on the point where the finger and thumb touch.

Move them together gently, then apart again. Just at the moment you feel them come together or separate, do you see an unexpected phenomenon? It's almost as if your hands are wet, and a thin film of water has collected around the point of contact between your thumb and forefinger.

Look for it as you move your fingers, and you'll see it, provided there's enough light shining through your fingers from behind and not too much illuminating the front side of them.

That alteration of the outline of your fingers is your personal Cosmic Energy field. Some people call it "the aura," others have different names: bioplasmic sheath, orgone field, life envelope, and the like. Call it what you wish: the important thing is that you've *seen* an energy field which is normally invisible.

VcToria Comments: If your third eye is open, you can stare at light as described above by Dad, and focus from that center point outwards. I find this easier to do if you look outside. Through a window, or sitting in the garden, or on your balcony. You will start to see dark and light movement that is fascinating to watch. That is the Universal energy.

My story: I was teaching a class of Reiki about 10 years ago. I was showing the students how to do this. One gentleman could not get it for quite a while. As I encouraged him, he suddenly exclaimed in glee "I see it, I see it". I cannot tell you how amazed he was, and also how impressed. Once you see it you can always see it without little effort. The idea is to not give up until you can do this.

NOW YOU ARE CONVINCED IT EXISTS, COSMIC ENERGY CAN BE DIRECTED BY YOUR OWN MIND VITALITY

The title of this section summarizes what this is all about. You *tune* yourself to Cosmic Energy, then *shape* and *direct* it with your mind. That's precisely what *New Avatar Power Secrets* do for you: show you the way to manipulate this energy which makes trees grow, birds fly, tides rise and fall, shapes mountains, and creates the world as we know it.

What you do is to let the Cosmos continue unfolding as it wishes, while you tap into a lode of Cosmic Energy and use it to shape your life. And the only shaping tool you need is your mind.

Does this have to be a well-educated, university-professor scientific Einstein-style mind? No, *it does not*. In fact, I've found the *less* you try to apply science, logic, and intellectual effort to *New Avatar Power,* the better the efforts. Not, I hasten to add, because *New Avatar Power* is unscientific and illogical, but because such analysis is unnecessary to the method.

By all means check out *New Avatar Power* later and find it's pure and simple alignment with Natural Law, but *first* clear up life's hassles with it.

You're capable of reading these words. That's sufficient for you to make use of *New Avatar Power Secrets*. If I was forced to make a choice, I would suggest a person who has *not* had a university education nor even graduated from high school is the one most likely to succeed with *New Avatar Power.*

COSMIC ENERCY IS THE MOST POWERFUL FORCE IN THE UNIVERSE

You'll have realized by now what a dynamite energy you're getting to control. This Cosmic Energy which spreads to the furthermost stars is *in control*: it shapes the present and the future with its immutable laws.

Yet you have this God-given tool to carve the results the way you want them to be: applying your mind as *New Avatar Power Secrets* suggest, this roaring torrent of Cosmic Power becomes a pussycat of cooperation, bending easily to your bidding.

Right at this very moment you're like a swimmer, about to find a swift current going the way you want to go. Trying to swim *against* the tide is exhausting, even painful. Finding the right channel to move along makes life easy, effortless, and progressive.

That's where you're going: tuning to *New Avatar Power* by using the *Secrets* puts you slapbang in the middle of a future shaping current—*and you decide where you wish to go.*

So what are we waiting for? Listen: we're *not* waiting. You're already on your way, even if you have yet to notice. You began the process when you opened this book. Nothing's changed, you say? Stay with me: your personal miracles are coming closer by the minute.

NEW AVATAR POWER IS HOLY AND PURE

Sadly, for reasons best left uninvestigated, some sincerely religious people will tell you that using Cosmic Energy, *New Avatar Power*, or similar psychic powers is "The Work of the Devil."

If that is your firm belief, or even your vague worry, I'd be the last to alter your religious convictions (provided you don't ask me to alter mine to line up with yours).

I will make two replies to those who suggest that the use of psychic power is somehow evil or undesirable. I believe these two statements as sincerely as the denigrators of psychic power hold to their beliefs. Then I'll rest my case, and you must reach your own decisions on who is right and who is wrong.

1. If psychic power is the Devil's work, then you *believe* in a Devil, and by extension, you believe in God. On your ground, then, the greatest Book ever written had God's Son tell mankind (St. John, 14, v. 12): "The works that I do shall he do also; and greater works than these shall he do." And Jesus is the finest example of using Cosmic Energy (Godpower) to work miracles—whether healing or feeding a multitude with loaves and fishes. Does that sound like the Devil's work, or any kind of ban against working personal miracles?

2. *New Avatar Power* is an updating of psychic power methods which were drawn from similar sources to the Bible, which is, of course, Judaic in origin. The techniques of *New Avatar Power* are aligned with old Hebrew religious and mystic teachings. They bear no resemblance to, nor are they drawn from, Black Magic or similar negative and destructive sources.

NEW AVATAR POWER WELCOMES AN AIMING POINT

If you have a plant growing in a pot and it needs water, do you carefully pour water on the soil around its stem, or do you stand on the other side of the room with a hose set on wide spray and while watering the plant, also water the chairs, table, TV, stereo, and carpet?

Sounds like a stupid question with an obvious answer, right? So it may seem—yet both methods get water to the plant, even if the spray technique takes longer and wets things which hardly require it.

Apply a similar thought to *New Avatar Power Secrets*. Yes, you can apply a "spray" aim and ask the energy "I want to be happy." You'll end up happy, but it can take a while, and lots of other things (which you may or may not agree with) will happen in-between.

Better to give the energy a point to aim at, without getting too specific. *New Avatar Power* works best if you request, for example, "I would like enough money to get out of debt and have enough over to indulge in some luxuries."

There's a fine line to observe here. *New Avatar Power* begins to lose efficiency if you insist: "I want to win *this* lottery on *that* day, bringing in exactly $50,000." There's a neat tightrope to walk, by being specific enough to let *New Avatar Power* know what you want, but allowing it to bring it to you in its own efficient way—*which can be unexpectedly different from what you thought was easiest and best.*

FIRST SECRET OF NEW AVATAR POWER

Right up top of your *New Avatar Power* plans, here is the first important secret to keep in mind: **Use** *New Avatar Power* **to bring things to you. That's more efficient than trying to send things away.**

You'll understand the logic of this later in this book. Because of the way *New Avatar Power* operates, it's far simpler to *create* than it is to destroy with this power. Cosmic Energy can do either—read reports on the next hurricane or earthquake! But your control, using your mind, is much surer when you're bringing items into your life, rather than trying to banish something physical.

CHANGE IS THE KEY TO USING NEW AVATAR POWER

Are you unhappy? In pain? Disturbed? Dissatisfied? Unfulfilled? Distressed? Harassed?

I'll ask you, what would cure that? Without going into any specifics, the one-word answer is "Change." To improve your life you need to change present conditions. Ridiculously simple: if things stay the same, you'll stay frustrated and depressed. Change—the right change, of course, not any old change—will remove the problems, enabling you to blossom like a beautiful flower.

WHAT NEEDS CHANGING IN YOUR LIFE?

Here is one of your early *New Avatar Power* decision points. We know you need to change your life. Now I'm going to help you decide what needs changing, and how to do it.

In your present existence, what would you like to change? More importantly, what needs changing *first*, assuming it cannot all be done in one sweeping step, and what are you aiming for after the change has happened?

As you consider those questions, keep the **First Secret** in mind. It's important, even if it was not the deep and arcane piece of spooky wisdom you might have been expecting! We'll be suggesting how to place your *New Avatar Power* on a firm aiming foundation. That forms a vital part of your *Mystic Initiation*.

YOUR MYSTIC INITIATION

New Avatar Power, works best if it is given the go-ahead to achieve definite goals. Your *Mystic Initiation* thus becomes the next exciting step toward total fulfillment and happiness.

Keeping the **First Secret** in mind, what are you going to request *New Avatar Power* to do for you first?

Say, some of you are thinking, what's so mystic about all that? Where are the robes and incense, the meditation, the candles and tar, the calls to Hidden Beings, the Words of Mighty Power, and all the rest of a Mystic Ceremony?

You can, if you wish, add any physical symbols to this Initiation, but there is no necessity so to do. If you wish to set the stage with such arcane accoutrements, do so by all means, and be happy. But realize they are what they are: stage-dressing, a background to something which is going on at deep levels of your mind, which really needs no outer manifestations to make it work.

And the language I invite you to use for this Initiation is twentieth century. Agreed, you *can* call on Mystic Beings in their own languages of the Middle Ages and earlier, but for the moment we're talking to you and your inner mind which have been formed in *this* century.

So let's set up conditions, and if they look different from what you were expecting, alter any conditions you wish which will make you feel comfortable.

But the central objective is to decide on *changes*. Into your mind we are about to place the idea of change, this being the key to making life more harmonious. And while we're planting the idea, we'll also decide what needs to come to you *soon* to make the most desirable and pressing changes take place.

Relationships with others fouled up? Home life unhealthily sad? Children out of control? Investments failing? Job insecure or objectionable? Marriage out of kilter? Enemies bugging you? Health down? Status shaky? Lonely? Bored with life? Social scene not to

INITIATION TO NEW AVATAR POWER

your liking? Personality kinks need curing? Suffering from indefinite fears?

Those are just a few areas to get you thinking about what's wrong with your life. Quite obviously, we need to clearly identify what's *wrong* before we can initiate changes to put things *right*.

Write *down everything which is wrong with your life*. This part of your *Mystic Initiation* brings your problems up front, out in the open. No need to write a whole book: just a few words identifying each separate problem will do fine. Everything which upsets your current peace of mind goes on this list. And I do mean everything, from your biggest problems, right down to the lady at work who annoys you with that twitching eyebrow. Worry, problem, irritation, aggravation, minor annoyance—get them all written down.

Now number them in order of priority. And that can be a problem in itself! Many people have so many worries, they're puzzled as to which is biggest.

Mark the figure "1" against the problem which worries you most, the one which needs to be cured first. The one which gets you steamed up or depressed, and occupies your thoughts more than any of the others.

Have you identified it? Now here's the next vital tip: *Assume that No. 1 has been cured,* and look at the remainder of the list. If the one marked No. 1 *didn't exist*, which would be the problem at the top of the list for action? Mark "2" beside that one. Then pretend *that* one doesn't exist, and proceed to No. 3.

Go on like that, mentally canceling the pressing items in order until your whole list has been numbered. Maybe your list runs from 1 to 5, maybe it runs from 1 to 365—no matter. You've taken a vast stride toward helping yourself: *New Avatar Power* now knows what it has to tackle.

On a fresh sheet of paper, write down the numbers of your problems, one number to a line. Now indicate how you wish to solve each problem. Remember the **First Secret**: *Solve problems by bringing things to you.*

Looking at No. 1 on your list, what item brought to you would solve it? Most people will have money worries highest on their list. So alongside No. 1 write the amount necessary to make that problem go away, if you had the money right now. Just the right amount, no extra dollars for a tank of gas for the car—presumably keeping the car running would be lower down the list, if that was a problem.

Getting the picture? Specifically, you must break your problems down into bite-size pieces. You may have been tempted to write: "No. 1: Pay all debts."

Could be okay, but it would be better to be a little more precise. Some of your debts must be more pressing than others: more accurately, you might have written: "No. 1: Bring rent up to date," while "Pay telephone account" could be much lower down the list.

I've purposely chosen money as an example, because it's easy to identify. Emotional problems can be more of a challenge. But, with thought, you can figure what needs to come to you to solve any problem.

VcToria Comments: Although I agree with Dad on his money comments, I do not agree on that being No. 1 on your list. You need to find 'peace and harmony' within yourself. Once you have harmonious energy, you can magnify the shifts without having worry as a constant nagging feeling.

ONWARD, THROUGH THE BRONZE DOOR

The *Iron Door*, often the one most firmly closed to many people is behind you. No matter how rusty the hinges were, you've eased it open, and you're ready to proceed to the next chapter and bring tremendous life-changing miracles another splendid step closer.

SUMMARY OF CHAPTER 1

1. Read the whole book before starting your *New Avatar Power* program.
2. *New Avatar Power* (Cosmic Energy) is all around you. You're going to use it to put things right in your life.
3. Reinforce your belief in Cosmic Energy by hearing and seeing it.
4. You're tuning yourself to Cosmic Energy, and using *New Avatar Power Secrets* to shape and direct it to change your existence. You need no accessories: your mind is the only required tool.
5. You do *not* need to be well-educated to use *New Avatar Power*.
6. You decide what you wish to become, where you wish to go, to make you supremely content.
7. *New Avatar Power* has nothing to do with the Devil and His Works.
8. *New Avatar Power* welcomes an aiming point.
9. **First Secret**: Use *New Avatar Power* to bring things to you.
10. Define your problems in your *Mystic Initiation* list.
11. Establish their priorities and write down desired solutions.

Inside The Bronze Door: Your Confidential Corporeal Avatar Commands

2

INSIDE THE BRONZE DOOR: YOUR CONFIDENTIAL CORPOREAL AVATAR COMMANDS

New Avatar Power works at many levels, whether visible or invisible. Materially, emotionally, mentally, and spiritually, these *Secrets* are part of your mind, body and soul.

This chapter is concerned with the material plane, the area of life you can see, touch, taste, smell, and hear. In keeping with our picture of entering the Four Doors of the Castle, this is where you pause in the courtyard and prepare yourself before approaching the *Silver Door.*

PHYSICAL TENSION MAY IMPEDE NEW AVATAR POWER

The foaming, exhilarating tide of Cosmic Energy operates like any other flow of natural energy or fluid. It seeks the line of least resistance: it would rather flow "downhill" than "uphill," and if it meets an obstruction it will divide and flow past, rather than wasting vitality trying to go through.

You're tuning yourself to be a channel for Cosmic Energy, and if you represent an obstruction to the easy flow of the energy, it will tend to bypass you, and you'll have less than you should to work your life-changing miracles.

Several ways exist for you to impede this tide, but the primary cause can be physical. In order for your mind to shape and control Cosmic Energy, your physical body needs to be relaxed.

The reason, briefly stated, is that every muscle in your body gives off electric currents when that muscle is tense, and when many muscles are tightly tied in knots, the resulting surge of random electricity somehow interferes with the free flow of Cosmic Energy.

So whenever you start out to work with *New Avatar Power*, your first action is to relax physically. That's the main theme of this chapter, and mastering the simple technique which uses what I've called your *Confidential Corporeal Commands* will automatically and easily open you up as a Cosmic Energy channel.

CORPOREAL AVATAR COMMANDS

HOW TO BANISH CONDITIONS WHICH SLOW DOWN YOUR NEW AVATAR POWER

We're opening the Bronze Door for you, remember? Working in the material plane, with your physical body, you're about to discover how to open yourself up to the glittering flow of *New Avatar Power*. You'll *feel* it filtering through your body, and know that you're demolishing physical barriers which have so far prevented the energy from working its impressive miracles for you.

The process is simple and easy to apply, takes up only a few minutes of your time, and is unique to you: you're about to acquire a personal technique which no one else has or uses quite the same as you do. It's a personal key to opening that Bronze Door, and enables you to do what no one else can: transform you into a free-running channel for the miracle-working vitality of *New Avatar Power*.

YOUR CONFIDENTIAL CORPOREAL COMMANDS

No need to be scared of that 29-letter title. You're going to *use* it, not have to say it. What does it mean? *Confidential*: secret, personal, for your eyes and ears only. *Corporeal*: material, physical, bodily. *Commands*: authorize, control, rule.

You're about to discover, then, a personal bodily control which is applied by saying or thinking a few simple words.

First we'll create your *Confidential Corporeal Commands*, then I'll tell you how and when to use them. As I promised, they're unique to *you*: *no other reader* has the same way of using these words as you do, and very few will even have the same words. This way, you gain the very maximum benefit, simply be-

CORPOREAL AVATAR COMMANDS

cause these *Commands* are matched accurately to your mind and body.

What's your first name? Not necessarily the one on your birth certificate. You may have been named Stanley or Elizabeth by your parents. Chances are most people know you as Stan or Betty.

What we're looking for is the name you answer to most readily, or even one you'd *like* to be called. The important feature is that you must feel comfortable with the name you build your *Confidential Corporeal Commands* from.

It's the name your best friend would call you if you were on a relaxed trip, and he or she had found something exciting for you to share.

"Hey, *Stan*: come look at this tremendous view."

"Look, *Liz*, there's a deer under that tree."

Those sorts of names. Nicknames are fine: if lots of people call you "Bud," use that. But do not use a name which disturbs you even a little bit: some people close to you may call you "Fatso" or "Shorty." If you're totally at ease with that name, okay. But if you just go along with such a name, disliking it inside yourself, that is not the one to use.

Most people can at once identify the name they feel most comfortable with. If you have any problem deciding, set yourself up a "let's-pretend" scenario. If you had your druthers, what would you *like* people to call you, on a friendly basis?

No need to roll around the floor for three hours, wracking your brain on what name to use, weighing Jim against James or Jimmy; selecting Peggy, then deciding it's Peg, then rejecting both for Delilah! You can change this name usage at any time. In fact, as you alter your life circumstances, it's best if you do change the name to line up with your new image.

You've selected your name. Now what's the first letter, the initial, of your *family* name? Single or mar-

CORPOREAL AVATAR COMMANDS

ried name: your *present* name—the one you sign on a cheque or banker's draft. The name you filled in when you ordered this book. The name you write when someone says, "Please sign here."

If you think I'm hedging this around more than somewhat, you're right, I am! I *know* some people will put up unnecessary obstacles to *themselves*. Why? For deep psychological reasons too complex to air here, but suffice to say some readers (not you, I trust) will spend days deciding what initial letter I'm talking about here.

"I was born Wadlkowski, my father simplified it to Vaddelkov, but a computer spelled it Faddelkov so some of my charge cards are in that name. Others are in my married name, which is Smith, but my present common-law husband is called Brown (when he's not calling himself De Haviland for business purposes). "What letter should I use?"

Maybe you think I'm kidding. I'm not: many similar letters in my filing cabinet show how that kind of turmoil will certainly stop a few of you in your tracks.

Handle it this way. If *today* you were to open a savings account, what would you answer when the teller asked: "What is your name?" If you *feel* like Mrs. Brown, that's it. If you still consider yourself Mrs. Smith, so be it. If you nurse an inner urge to resurrect the old family name, you're Wadlkowski. It's in *your* hands (and mind).

You now have an initial, plus the first name you fixed on. So you, Mrs. Elizabeth Jones, have decided on Betty J. You, Mr. Algernon Witherspoon, have adopted Rick W. (I'm not surprised).

Oh, dear. Yes, I hear you Ms. Van Der Hoof. Is your initial V, D, or H? Open the telephone book. Which letter is your name listed under? That's the one to use.

The third part of your *Confidential Corporeal Commands* is one word. That word is **Relax**. And the

CORPOREAL AVATAR COMMANDS

fourth and last part consists of the numbers from 1 to 10.

Putting together the whole of your *Confidential Corporeal Commands* goes: "Ten—Relax—(Name, Initial)........Nine—Relax—(Name, Initial)........Eight—Relax (Name, Initial).........." and so on down to ".........One—Relax—(Name, Initial)."

In place of "(Name, Initial)" you will, of course, use your own name and initial letter we've just so lengthily arrived at. Algernon Witherspoon, from the example above, would begin: "Ten—Relax, Rick W.—Nine..." and so on.

That's your complete and individual *Confidential Corporeal Commands*. Say yours over a couple of times to get the hang of it. Realize that no one in this wide world says those words *exactly* as you do. A product of your own mind, those *Commands* are personally custom-built to have maximum effect.

VcToria Comments: Even I found that long and tedious to have been explained that way. Why he did not say I use "Ten—Relax, Geof G." I will never know. My name is VcToria Gray and I use "Ten—Relax, VcToria G."

[Even though I am about to add the 'Cobb' back to my last name I would still just use G.]

WHEN TO USE YOUR CONFIDENTIAL CORPOREAL COMMANDS

Chapter Four explains how your *Corporeal Commands* fit into the whole *New Avatar Power* method which is going to change your life to happiness and pleasure. You'll be using the *Commands* on a daily basis.

But that's not their only use. You can employ them to your definite advantage whenever and wherever

CORPOREAL AVATAR COMMANDS

you're in a pressure situation. You can easily recognize when you're reacting to harassment or danger by the tension which builds in you, often beginning in the pit of your stomach.

Mentally (not aloud) reciting your *Confidential Corporeal Commands* will release the tensions, and you'll sail cheerfully through many situations which previously got you literally "uptight." Try it next time you feel anger rising or irritation growing: you could be amazed.

Usually, one run through of the complete commands is sufficient, but repeating the process several times will do you no harm at all. Good practice, in fact!

IMPORTANT FIRST NEW AVATAR POWER STEPS

Get into the swing of your *Confidential Corporeal Commands*. They truly are opening you up to *New Avatar Power*, to allow that vital energy to work properly for you.

If convenient, find a few minutes each day to sit or lie down and run your *Commands* through your mind. It should take you almost a full minute to run through from 10 to 1. Slow your breathing, make it a bit deeper than usual, and time your *inhales* to coincide with the numbers. Thus you will be breathing in as you say "One," and breathing out as you slowly and distinctly think: "Relax (followed by your name and initial)."

After reaching the last words, lie or sit relaxed, letting your mind run free for a few seconds or even minutes before you go about your business.

Where you do this is unimportant, although it would be nice if you had a regular quiet corner to practice in. Conditions should be as peaceful as you can make them without upsetting normal routines. It would be an error, for instance, to insist on your children

CORPOREAL AVATAR COMMANDS

switching off their stereo while you practice. Detach from the racket by using your *Commands* instead.

Best results usually come if you recite your *Commands* with eyes closed, but again, it's up to you. Do it the way which feels most comfortable for you.

SIGNS THAT YOUR CONFIDENTIAL CORPOREAL COMMANDS ARE WORKING

How do you know when your inner self is paying attention to your *Confidential Corporeal Commands* and opening up to let *New Avatar Power* come rushing in?

You'll *feel* it, that's how. Different people get different effects: but you must feel *some* effects every time you recite the *Commands* before going on with the rest of the *New Avatar Power* techniques.

If your *Confidential Corporeal Commands* produce *none* of the following effects, practice regularly until they do. Proceeding from this point to open the *Silver Door* will be useless until the *Confidential Corporeal Commands* are drilled into your conscious and subconscious minds.

You should detect any of the following. If you detect all of them that will be great, but just detecting one is all that is needed to move onwards to the *Silver Door*.

1. Prickling of the hands, feet or limbs.
2. Tickling in your forehead.
3. A feeling that the room has become lighter or darker, even though the lighting remains the same.
4. A faint sweet odor around you.
5. A sensation that someone is standing close to you.
6. Sounds around you becoming distinctly fainter *or* louder.
7. An extra flow of saliva in your mouth.

At least one of the above shows you that your *Confidential Corporeal Commands* are becoming effective. There's no need to sit or lie like a petrified mummy while you're doing all this. If you itch, scratch it. If you want to cough or sneeze, go ahead. If your body feels it wants to move to a different position, move it.

START MAKING LIFE EASIER WITH YOUR CONFIDENTIAL CORPOREAL COMMANDS

We've seen the *Commands* in action for some people already, but please do not think that's all there is to mastering *New Avatar Power*.

VcToria Comments: My dad is referring to the 'testimonials' that are in the original book. As I have stated many times in the previously re-published books I have removed these.

On the contrary, you are more likely to need the rest of the technique. So refrain from throwing this book in the garbage pail if this is all you've done so far, and your life has yet to turn to magnificent success and brilliance.

What you can do most definitely is use the *Commands* you're mastering to get physically more comfortable. Aches and pains vanish like magic if you flop down on a couch and mentally recite your *Commands*. Even migraines will fade away for some people. Try your *Commands* on your insomnia next time you're lying blinking at the dark ceiling. Next thing you'll know it's daybreak, and the alarm's going off in your ear!

At the dentist, recite your *Commands* as the sizzling drill comes closer. Amazing! You hardly felt a thing.

Feet ache? Muscles sore from a work-out? Elbow throbbing from a blow? Recite your *Commands* and feel

CORPOREAL AVATAR COMMANDS

the pain ebb away—although if you've suffered damage which needs medical aid, you'll also make an appointment with the healer of your choice.

Question: If *New Avatar Power* is so good, why go to a doctor to get well? *Answer:* *New Avatar Power* is intended to make you harmonious and happy, but it's an arcane truth that if something can be accomplished physically, it's more efficient to do it that way than to attempt to make psychic power do all the work.

Yes, *New Avatar Power* has some remarkable healings to its credit, but until you master its use completely, you'd do better to rely on normal treatment for life's ailments.

And how will you know when *New Avatar Power* is truly your servant? Simple: you'll have acquired everything you need, and you'll be so neatly into the swing of Natural Law that you won't *need* a doctor: your body will have healed itself, you'll be bursting with vitality, and the whole world will be rosy.

SECOND SECRET OF NEW AVATAR POWER: THE FABULOUS FEAR ERADICATOR

The most corrosive and impeding emotion which stops many people from achieving their full potential is fear. Fear of being broke, fear of the boss, fear of the unknown; the dictionary is filled with phobias which describe the various fears we are assailed by.

Morbid dislike of heights, open spaces, cats, pain, men, women, storms, being alone, crowds, enclosed spaces, dogs, spiders, crossing streets, sex, being touched, blood, water, mice, dirt, new things, the dark, snakes, light, food, being buried alive, death, poison, strangers, and even falling asleep, is only a partial list of our fears. If anything can be imagined, someone fears it.

CORPOREAL AVATAR COMMANDS

New Avatar Power enables you to clean out that impediment to easy living, in three simple steps.

1. Identify your fears.
2. Apply the *Fabulous Fear Eradicator* to them.
3. See those fears dissolve and vanish like ghosts at cockcrow.

Just like your *Mystic Initiation* list of problems, make a list of your fears (in fact, it's quite likely, if a fear is strong enough, you may have already included it on your problem list. No matter: a problem attacked from several directions will vanish quicker).

This is merely a list of your fears, arranged in descending order of strength, which you're making. Unlike your problem list, there's no need to suggest solutions: the *Fabulous Fear Eradicator* will take care of that.

Ready to use it? So find five or ten spare minutes, sit or lie down in the quiet, and recite your *Confidential Corporeal Commands*.

Having reached the last "Relax," sit quietly with eyes closed for a full minute. While you're sitting there, pretend someone is setting up a chalkboard (green or black, whichever you please) just in front of you. If you disliked school, and the idea of a chalkboard is disturbing, imagine a movie screen. And if you don't like movie houses because of the crowds or the dark, imagine instead that a TV is before you.

All you're doing, in your mind, is setting up a frame, whether it's the imaginary border of the board, or the edges of the movie or TV screen.

Call Fear No. 1 to mind. If it's a thing you fear, such as spiders or an animal, pretend a clear picture of that *thing* has appeared on the board or screen. It is unable to touch you, of course, because it's a representation of your mind, and stays where it is. But try your

CORPOREAL AVATAR COMMANDS

hardest to make believe your most virulent fear is depicted on your chosen screen or board. The mind work should be sufficiently powerful to make you actually *feel* fearful, even though you know you're quite safe.

If your fear is a situation, or something intangible, like fear of the dark, pretend you're looking at a picture of *yourself* in exactly the situation or circumstance which you fear. Again, set up the thoughts so you sense the situation, and feel the tendrils of terror touching you.

Now, when the picture is firmest in your mind, pretend you are reaching out to clear the board, switch off the movie projector, or punch the "Off" button on the television. The fear picture dissolves, disappears.

Now fish around in your memory, and replace the picture in front of you with a playback of a situation which you truly enjoyed. Could be a ballgame, an outing to the beach, a romp with the kids or your lover: something you vividly recall and enjoyed tremendously at the time.
And that's it. Open your eyes when you're ready, and carry on doing whatever needs doing.

That simple technique will work. Even practicing it once, you'll find the next time your "fear" situation occurs, you're less scared by it. Daily use of the *Fabulous Fear Eradicator* will change you tremendously: you'll find to your amazement that things which scared the living daylights out of you no longer have the power to even cause you to suffer a single goose-bump!

If you're deathly afraid of spiders right now, after using the *Fabulous Fear Eradicator* you may never find them attractive, but you will discover the biggest, hairiest, skitteringest, blackest spider can walk over your foot, and all you will feel is a mild distaste, or even interest in the creature. And having tackled and taken the edge off Fear No. 1, proceed to dispel Fear No. 2. It gets easier as you go down the list, and if you need to return for a refresher treatment for No. 1, eventually you find yourself in the delightful position of having nothing left to fear.

The feeling of freedom that it brings is indescribable.

THIRD SECRET OF NEW AVATAR POWER: THE EXTRAORDINARY HAPPINESS RESTORER

Feeling down? Not all the time, maybe, but in waves, at intervals, maybe geared to the phases of the Moon, maybe not.

Everyone has times when he feels unhappy for no good reason. Well, almost everybody: you may be one of the lucky souls who *never* feels unhappy, but if so, why did you buy this book?

Assuming you get these waves of depression, of varying depths and at varying intervals, here's the *New Avatar Power Secret* to cure that undesirable condition.

The *Extraordinary Happiness Restorer* needs no explanation: it does exactly what it says, simply, easily, and quickly, turning sadness into happiness as automatically as switching on a light.

The setup is identical to the *Fabulous Fear Eradicator*. Again, when you have five or ten minutes to spare, sit or lie down in the quietest place you can find and recite your *Confidential Corporeal Commands.*

As before, sit with your eyes closed and imagine your board or screen in front of you. Now do the same as you did *after* you dissolved the "fear" picture: use your memory to playback on the screen of your mind a situation where you were truly happy.

Aw, come on! You must have *one* happy memory, even if you have to go back years in your mind.

You really and truly don't have a single happy memory to put onto your screen? So be it: then pretend (and this is very much second best and will need work-

CORPOREAL AVATAR COMMANDS

ing several times) that you're watching other people having a happy time *and one of them is you.*

Got the picture this time? Do not wipe the board, turn off the projector or switch off the imaginary TV. Run right through the episode in your mind. If it's a brief one, rerun it a couple of times. Allow yourself to get immersed in it. Smile.

Now repeat your *Confidential Corporeal Commands* one time. Stay relaxed for a minute or so, then go about your business. You'll be amazed at the lift in your spirits.

A closing thought. Whenever I mention a specific length of time in my writings, someone writes to say it's not long enough, or too short. Twice now in recent pages I've referred to "five or ten minutes"; I've also referred to "a full minute" and "a minute or so." Approximate times only: use as much or as little time as you wish. But don't mentally gabble your way through the processes, trying to squeeze the whole thing into a few seconds.

And even though you've been doing a great deal of mental work, the chief effects have been physical. If you've found tangible effects with your *Confidential Corporeal Commands*, you're ready to turn to the next chapter with me and open the *Silver Door* to fascinating mental vistas.

SUMMARY OF CHAPTER 2

1. This chapter has dealt chiefly with physical matters, such as bodily relaxation.
2. *New Avatar Power* works best when it has a clear channel to flow through.
3. You can impede *New Avatar Power* if you're tense.

CORPOREAL AVATAR COMMANDS

4. *Confidential Corporeal Commands*, a few personal, simple words, *attuned to you alone*, will allow you to become a channel for *New Avatar Power*.
5. Work with your *Commands* a few minutes each day if convenient.
6. *Feel* your *Commands* working *before going on to the next chapter*.
7. *Confidential Corporeal Commands* can be used to dispel pain.
8. Use the *Fabulous Fear Eradicator* until you fear nothing.
9. When you're less happy than you'd like to be, employ the *Extraordinary Happiness Restorer*.

Behind The Silver Door: The Wonders Of Mysterious Avatar Power Words

3

BEHIND THE SILVER DOOR: THE WONDERS OF MYSTERIOUS AVATAR POWER WORDS

Welcome, traveler. You've passed the *Iron* and *Bronze Gates*, proven to yourself the existence of *New Avatar Power*, learned a *Secret* or two, and opened yourself up physically as a smooth and efficient *New Avatar Power* channel.

It will come as no surprise to you to learn that as well as physical impediments, *New Avatar Power* is also sensitive to mental obstacles.

THOUGHTS AND WORDS CAN BE IMPEDING VIBRATIONS

New Avatar Power, you're aware, exists at all levels of your being, and it's most concentrated at mind levels, within your mental paths. Just as physical tension can cause the tides of *New Avatar Power* to flow around, instead of through you, *so certain words and thoughts can have an identical effect.*

FOURTH SECRET OF NEW AVATAR POWER: THE MYSTERIOUS "N'T" WORDS

To all those people who wrote and said "It Doesn't Work," my sincere and abiding thanks. Without your letters we might never have uncovered this *Fourth Secret*.

With your letters beside me, I asked myself what is the common thread, the identical feature, which may be preventing *New Avatar Power* from working its stupendous miracles for these few unfortunates?

I used my own *New Avatar Power* techniques to fathom the answer. In a most satisfying revelation, I found out *what* was wrong, and if you're prepared to come with me into a little numerology, I found out *why* these people were not achieving success.

If, as each writer assured me, he had truly relaxed fully, then *New Avatar Power* must be blocked at some other level. And it turned out to be at the *mental* level, in a shape which had been staring me in the face.

For valid metaphysical and occult reasons, if a word which is written with the letters "N" and "T" separated by an apostrophe (to indicate a letter omitted

MYSTERIOUS AVATAR POWER WORDS

from that word) is regularly lying around in your mind paths, *New Avatar Power* will flow elsewhere because the word puts up a strong blockage to the energy.

Thus I discovered the *Mysterious N'T Words*: mysterious in their effects, not in the least mysterious in their meanings.

The N'T Words are ones like "can't," "won't," "doesn't," "isn't," "shouldn't"—any word where the three-letter word "not" has been shortened to "n't."

As simple as that, once uncovered. By thinking, saying, and writing "It *doesn't* work" the writers were putting up a very efficient *New Avatar Power* dam. No wonder it failed to work!

Why does such a simple word usage cause such a fantastic energy to flow elsewhere? The simple answer would be to say "That's just the way it is," and then set about curing the condition.

But for you people who would like a reason, let me (as previously indicated) cite a little numerology.

The word *Not* is useful, valuable, and carries a numerological total of 4. That's a fine solid number, and is usually connected with the material plane. Most prohibitions concern our physical conduct, and you'll find "not" throughout: "Thou shalt *not* steal," for instance, or "Do *not* pick the flowers." If they were rendered as "Thou shan't steal" and "Don't pick the flowers," I think you'll agree they lose some of their original impact.

Now the minute you drop the letter O from the word "not," as we do when we use the abbreviated "n't," the numerological total becomes, or tries to become 7. Seven is an occult mystic number, well suited to *New Avatar Power* and all psychic work. And I guess if N'T truly totaled 7 we'd have little to fuss about.

But it does not total 7: that apostrophe interrupts the totaling, and N'T stays as 5 (for the N) and 2 (for the T), kept at arms-length by the comma-in-the-air be-

67

tween them. Now 5 is the number of uncertainty, while 2 can be a decision number (Two choices, two paths at a fork in the road). Two is also the total of the word "No."

Thus, the combined occult effect of N'T words is to put up a sign which says simultaneously: *Uncertain, Decision*, plus overtones of a forbidding "No," as in "No Trespassing," "No Entry," "No Loitering," and other such phrases.

Recall that *New Avatar Power* takes the easiest path, and you can begin to understand when it comes to a channel carrying such signs (and because they're thoughts and words makes them no less effective), it turns aside and finds a clearer channel.

And if the preceding piece was all Greek to you, disregard it. Accept the "That's just the way it is," and let's find a simple way to clean up this blocked channel.

VcToria Comments: I have studied Numerology for years. I use it daily in my life. Particularly for the Personal Years [your own personal season as I like to call it]. If you are interested in a chart with all your own numbers and guidance, you can purchase this from my web store on my website: www.alternativeuniverse.ca

HOW TO BANISH THE MYSTERIOUS N'T WORDS

Consider the *Mysterious N'T Words* to be heavy transport and tracked vehicles, like bulldozers, traveling the channels of your mind. They'll soon chop the roadway into rough potholes and ruts, and the more of that type of traffic there is, the rougher the going is.

If you consider *New Avatar Power* as a finely tuned sports car, fast, and light, you can understand that it will find its own hassles in traveling such a route. So, on coming across such plowed up terrain,

MYSTERIOUS AVATAR POWER WORDS

New Avatar Power will merely take a fork in the road and go to its destination by another, smoother path.

So how are we going to get a crew out to repair the road, to make a channel which *New Avatar Power* will slide effortlessly along?

Luckily, the task is simple. The channel of your mind is self-repairing. Put up a sign which says "No Heavy Trucks. Tracked Vehicles Forbidden," and with the reduction in traffic of that kind, the ruts will automatically fill in, the corrugations will disappear, and your mind channel will become smooth and broad. At once, *New Avatar Power* will use such a route, and you get the benefits of this awesome power, latching onto it with the *Secrets* and working your life miracles.

Preventing this heavy traffic can be fun. It consists of playing the *Mysterious N'T Word Game*.

Is simpler than solitaire; requires the same number of players; can be played anywhere at any time; requires no board, cards, counters, dice, chips, apparatus, balls or space; and has one rule only. Nothing to buy, either!

Pretty neat game, eh? Playing it leads directly to making the smooth mental channel for *New Avatar Power* which it needs to bring your dreams to true and startling physical reality.

PLAYING THE MYSTERIOUS N'T WORD GAME

Number of players: one. That's you, as you may have realized. Played wherever and whenever you're thinking, talking, or writing—and it takes up no extra time. You play it in parallel with your day-to-day activities. And no accessories needed because it all goes on inside your head and mind.

Single rule: Whenever you find yourself thinking, saying or writing one of the *Mysterious N'T Words*, replace that word with a different word, or rephrase the thought to avoid the *N'T Word* altogether.

What was your reaction to that? Did you think, "I don't understand"? There you go: your very first opportunity to play! You thought the N'T word *"Don't."* Rethink the phrase. "I do not understand" would do as a replacement phrase—no N'T Word in that. But that's the easy way, and although it's not actually cheating to alter the N'T back to its original "Not," you'll get quicker results from the game if you also reduce the number of "Not's" in your thoughts and speech—they can so easily get slurred into N'T, can't they?

Oops! See that *Mysterious N'T Word* which slipped through my typewriter in the previous line? Banish it: I should have written: "They can so easily get slurred into N'T, agreed?"

A few examples will show you the simple ground rules.

"It doesn't work" can become "I have yet to see it work," or "It's failed to work so far."

"Don't touch!" can be phrased as "Do not touch!" or even better, "Keep your fingers off that!"

"I don't like him," becomes "I dislike him."

"We haven't got any," becomes "We have none."

Pretty simple, right? Yet the results are fantastic.

Now, please notice this is not intended to alter your entire way of talking. Playing the game and sounding like a Victorian poet is hardly the idea. For instance, if you habitually say, "I can't afford it," you're going to get some odd glances if you say instead, "I lack the wherewithal to make such a purchase." Sure, that sticks with the basic rule of the game, but it sounds kind of clumsy.

And the other point is that you aim to catch the N'T words *before* they get out into the open. Inside the privacy of your head you're at liberty to think things like, "I won't do it...rephrase without the N'T Word...I will not do it," but if you start inserting such changes into your speech or writing patterns, you'll impede communication with others.

So if you find you've said, "I haven't any idea," it's inadvisable to promptly bite your tongue and add: "I mean, I have no idea."

Catch the *Mysterious N'T Words* at their birth, in your mind (which is where the clearing up is going on), and you're playing the game right.

How do you know when you've won the game? By the stupendous things which start happening to you, as *New Avatar Power* sweeps through the new channel you've smoothed and brings your every last need and desire into your life in a rush of good fortune and happiness which can leave you breathless with amazement.

FIFTH SECRET OF NEW AVATAR POWER: THE SUPERB UNCERTAINTY BANISHER

You'll have realized that on the way to a new life, *New Avatar Power* requires you to make a decision or two. Deciding what's wrong with your life. Deciding which problem is the most important. Deciding what you wish to have happen to turn misery into delight.

Decisions! Decisions! And perhaps you're a person to whom decision-making comes hard. You can procrastinate for weeks, trying to fix on one of several alternatives.

You're in good company. "Maybe I should do such-and-so, or maybe something else would be better. Or perhaps the best might be to......" are trains of thought which haunt many people and can keep them chained to conditions which they desperately want to change. Yet until the decision is made and the wheels put into motion, life is likely to stay much the same.

Working with your *Mystic Initiation* list, for instance, will get much quicker results once you've made the "Bring me this and that" part also. If that portion of your *Mystic Initiation* is hedged around with alternatives, you're spreading *New Avatar Power* in all kinds of different directions and diluting the splendid effects which can come.

Here's glad news for you: the *Superb Uncertainty Banisher* propels you out of vacillating doubt and enables you to reach any decision between any number of alternatives, *automatically* and infallibly selecting the best one and rejecting the others. No more "I wonder what would happen if......". Instead, you have clear cut, firm direction which says: "Do this; forget about that, that and that."

You use a *New Avatar Power* technique to reach this decision point, so the results are always right for you. *New Avatar Power* unerringly takes you into the most harmonious possible conditions, even if the intervening steps may be totally unexpected.

Remember always that when *New Avatar Power* hands you a decision which you may wonder about, within your present circumstances, you're being propelled toward fulfillment and happiness, just as you set up the techniques of the *Secrets* to accomplish.

Here's how you do it. As before, find a quiet spot and recite your *Confidential Corporeal Commands*, just as you did to begin using the *Extraordinary Happiness Restorer*. Now, when it comes time to set up your board or screen, imagine pictures of whatever the various decisions are, from which you have to select one.

Pretend you're putting a picture of each one on your screen. Put up the first situation which could be a solution or a course to take. Then wipe it off (or mentally switch off the projector or turn off the TV). Replace the first picture with an alternative. Wipe that one. Put up the third, wipe it, and follow with any others until you've reviewed in your mind and on your mental screen all the alternatives which are possible. While

MYSTERIOUS AVATAR POWER WORDS

you're doing this, *remember what order you placed them in front of your mind.* Give them numbers: the first is No. 1, the second No. 2, and so on.

Here's where *New Avatar Power* makes the selection for you. In fact, it has already made the selection, even if you have yet to realize it. The most desirable solution is the *third* one you put on your screen, *if there were more than two alternatives to review.* If there were only two alternatives, the *second* one is the one to choose.

Accept that decision and go along with what *New Avatar Power* is suggesting. It works every time, and saves a lot of shilly-shallying and wondering what might happen if.

Use this simple process anytime you have a decision to make which involves several possible answers. Provided you've got your *Confidential Corporeal Commands* going well—and you were told not to proceed until you had—you're into a winning swing with the *Superb Uncertainty Banisher.*

SIXTH SECRET OF NEW AVATAR POWER: THE UNIQUE CREATIVITY REGENERATOR

Many people hanker after a career as an artist of some kind. Painting, photography, stage work, movie or TV involvements have a glamor which brings a thrill to living which is absent from many other more mundane pursuits.

And just as everyone can make use of *New Avatar Power* when they go about it the right way, so everyone has a streak of creativity within him, if he can only bring it out and make use of it.

Have you always figured you'd paint a masterpiece one day? Does writing the world's greatest novel interest you? How would you like to be free of day-to-day 9 to 5 routines, and enjoy the life of being a freelance writer? Or maybe you'd rather be in front of the cameras, winning the applause of the world. Or on stage, soaking up adulation?

Yes, you can do it—*if you use the right area of your natural creativity.* That's the challenge: you may battle for years to be a writer when your natural talent is to be a pianist. Or you may beat down the doors to producers' offices trying to be an actor or actress, when your creative streak is really aimed at oil painting.

And, of course, you may be like thousands of others who believe show-business people, artists, and writers are special people. "I'd love to try it, but I don't think I can," is the usual thought of many people.

Try it with *New Avatar Power.* You'll be amazed. All you have to do is go about the project in the right way. And even if the idea of your being creative has never entered your head, give this a try—you never know until you let *New Avatar Power* dig it up, exactly what your potentials are.

The *Unique Creativity Regenerator* simply and accurately uncovers your creative streak, enabling you to pursue it, develop it, and shine.

It begins just like the other Secrets. Recite your *Confidential Corporeal Commands* and pretend your board or screen is in front of you. (You should be getting well practiced at this by now!).

One of two ways you can go now. If you know for sure what your creative bent is, pretend to be an observer who is watching *you* doing your creative thing. Dig around in your memory and recreate your finest hour when you used your abilities to the full and earned applause. See yourself painting, acting, writing, producing—whatever. That's sufficient. Leave the picture on the screen as you open your eyes and carry on with whatever else you wish to do.

Now, what if you think you're as creative as a brick? Never even thought about show-business for yourself? Think you can't even draw a straight line?

You need to use the *Superb Uncertainty Banisher* to focus in on which area of creativity is for you. You know the routine. List the different areas of creative outputs and mentally put them up on your screen. The *third* one that *New Avatar Power* prompts you to consider is *the* one.

Pretend to blank your screen and take the final step. Think about how *you* would look if you were a success in the field you've chosen. Make it humorous if you like: you as an artist, complete with smock and floppy hat, splashing paint all over a giant canvas would be great.

Keep your thoughts light and lively: no gritting your teeth, creating deathly serious mind pictures!

Leave that thought on your screen as you open your eyes and carry on.

Simple? You bet! Natural Law is essentially simple and so is *New Avatar Power* as it aligns you with Natural Law. You'll be amazed.

SEVENTH SECRET OF NEW AVATAR POWER: DEFENDING YOURSELF WITH NEW AVATAR POWER

We need to look at one area of life which, no matter where you go, how high you soar, you'll have to contend with.

In fact the more progress you make, the more you'll fall prey to this condition, although it affects everyone at every strata of existence.

I'm referring to having enemies. Not necessarily people who actively hate you and will lurk in dark lanes waiting to hit you with an iron pipe. More insidious than that: I'm talking about those objectionable people, who out of malice or jealousy, will chip away at your peace of mind in a thousand sneaky ways, trying to destroy your hard-won peace of mind.

Perfectly servicable legal courses exist to stop people who are obviously attacking you, but what about the emotional and mental tortures which your foes can inflict on you?

That's where you need the *Seventh Secret of New Avatar Power*. As usual, it's simple, quick—and amazingly effective.

Recite your *Confidential Corporeal Commands*. Erect your familiar mental screen or board. Now pretend that from out of the framework are coming *big black arrows*. Each one represents a disturbance which is being sent at you by people who dislike you. Think of these arrows as being something like a flock of slow-flying crows, winging toward you.

Think of a chain-saw, a circular saw, a hand-saw—any kind of saw which you've either handled, seen in a store, or looked at pictured in a catalog.

Pretend the saw is fixed up at the edge of your screen, and as each arrow comes through the screen, the saw moves across and *chews the arrow into dust*. You can see that picture in your mind, right?

End of instructions. End of torment. Doing that a number of times on a daily basis will have startling results. The people who were bugging you may seem to be doing the same old things, trying their tired tricks to annoy, hurt or destroy you, but *they'll fail*.

New Avatar Power comes to your aid, and you find yourself untouchable. Happier, more peaceful, and able to make progress which was missing before.

NEW AVATAR POWER LEADS UNERRINGLY TO A NEW SUPERLATIVE WAY OF LIFE FOR YOU

Carried along joyously on this tide of expectations and hopes, this is the moment to slow down and

MYSTERIOUS AVATAR POWER WORDS

look at where you're heading. What exactly is this book all about? Can it do what it promises?

Sober thought: this *book* can do nothing but be a couple of hundred paper pages between covers. But the words on these pages, knitting with your thoughts and actions will carry you to heights which are literally only limited by your imagination.

If you can think of it, *New Avatar Power* will create it for you. Health, wealth, and happiness are yours with *New Avatar Power Secrets*. All this book asks of you is that you flow with its suggestions and follow the directions as they are spelled out. Then come the amazing results, with the added satisfaction of knowing that *you* did it for yourself.

Which raises a point from people who have read my previous book, *The Miracle of New Avatar Power*. In that book each technique called, by name, on *Mystic Beings* to aid in the miracles. Why are they not in these pages?

Believe me, they are! Calling the Names of Beings is one way of attuning yourself to particular areas of Cosmic Energy to bring changes in your life. The drawback to such "calling" is that, when printed on a page, the *pronunciation* can be in doubt for people who believe that's ultimately important.

So *New Avatar Power Secrets* use a different method of attuning you to the Mystic areas of Power: instead of calling Names, you use your own "tuning abilities."

That's exactly what the *Confidential Corporeal Commands* and (from the next chapter) your *Personal Verbal Seals* are doing: aligning you with Unseen Energies exactly as other methods do, and somewhat more efficiently, because one area of doubt has been removed. You're using your own thoughts and voice, putting your own key into the Doors to Cosmic Energy, instead of asking Other Powers to do it for you.

EARLY SIGNS THAT NEW AVATAR POWER IS DOING ITS MARVELOUS WORK

Let's assume you're on your second run through this book. You've read it through once, as suggested, to see what it's all about—and you have *not*, I sincerely trust, tried to pick little bits out here and there because you thought you'd give it a try. Once again I repeat the important warning: dipping will impede excellent results.

So you've reached this stage, having carried out the exercises so far. Yes, they are exercises: just as you would physically work with muscles to get them toned up, so the repetition of, for example, your *Confidential Corporeal Commands* tones up your psychic "muscles."

At this stage, some people will have seen instant miracles. That new car, new home, perfect lover, promotion, or desired change will already have flown to you, borne on the wings of *New Avatar Power* as it courses through your life and environment, obeying your tiniest wish.

But maybe you're still waiting for miracles to happen. That's okay: if you've followed through on the directions, your personal miracles are in the Cosmic Machine. You can *feel* them coming, even if they're not tangible in the material plane yet.

Feel them? Yes, I mean that literally. Spend a few moments, right now, reciting your *Confidential Corporeal Commands*. Compare how you feel before you start them with how you feel when you reach the last "Relax."

Notice the new energy flowing through you? The fresh, calm strength? The lessening of uptightness? The peacefulness within your mind?

That represents destiny preparing you for the better times to come. These feelings are just the thin edge of the wedge, the tiniest fraction of the joy, overflowing happiness and total satisfaction and peace of mind which will be yours when *New Avatar Power* has swung fully into your life to bring you the possessions, relationships, and environment which are your Cosmic Birthright.

Inevitably, with the precision and accuracy of fine clockwork, you're turning life's tide to go *your* way. *New Avatar Power* knows the smoothest possible path to happiness. Ride the tide, and savor the growing fulfillment of it all.

SUMMARY OF CHAPTER 3

1. This chapter realigns mental paths to open you to the tide of *New Avatar Power.*
2. Thoughts and words can impede *New Avatar Power*
3. Recognize the *Mysterious N'T Words* and banish them in a simple game.
4. Use the *Superb Uncertainty Banisher* to reach difficult decisions, *automatically.*
5. You can amaze yourself with the *Unique Creativity Regenerator*, even if you've never thought of yourself as creative in the least.
6. Enemies are no longer a problem when you use the *Seventh Secret of New Avatar Power.*
7. The Mystic Beings of my previous book have not gone. They're even closer, and you need not even learn their names.
8. Practice *feeling New Avatar Power* flowing through you.

Beyond The Golden Door: Your Personal Avatar Verbal Seals

4

BEYOND THE GOLDEN DOOR: YOUR PERSONAL AVATAR VERBAL SEALS

We've worked on physical planes at the *Iron* and *Bronze Doors*. Your mental planes have been shaped and smoothed inside the *Silver Door*. You're now ready to take the next step: working with emotional, spiritual, and true Hidden Planes to tie the three areas of working into a logical and powerful whole.

WHAT YOUR PERSONAL VERBAL SEALS CAN DO FOR YOU

As you've noticed, I frequently invite you to "see" yourself doing or being something. Pretend such-and-so is happening. So far it's been simple, but we're coming to a stage where I invite you to pretend you're in situations which you have never experienced. That could be a challenge, if it were not for your *Personal Verbal Seals*.

These simple phrases are once again keyed to you, perfectly matched to your thinking patterns, by the logical process of using *your* mind to create them.
We know many powerful phrases, incantations, and prayers exist which can work miracles. Yet their drawback can be that they fail to quite fit the way your mind operates.

For instance, the well-known technique of Transcendental Meditation, which you've no doubt heard of, employs phrases known as mantras to help the student of that technique reach deep meditation.

The mantras are phrases matched by experienced instructors to the student. Each student is told his or her mantra, and has to promise never to reveal it to anyone else.

That method works—but it does rely on the instructor being right every time with his choice of mantra for the particular student.

So here we carry that method a step further. So that the words, pronunciation, and delivery match *perfectly* to you, with no chance of error, *you* create the phrases which I have called your *Personal Verbal Seals*.

There can be no error. I show you, step by step, how to put your phrases together. *You* select the words from your own experience and vocabulary. The end results are words and phrases which are more powerful and accurate than any Names of Mystic Beings or

Mantras or Spells anyone else can hand you—*because you created them yourself.*

DECIDE ON YOUR ADMIRATION TARGETS

Whom do you admire most in this whole wide world at the moment? Could be a movie star, a president, a historical character, a friend, even the guy who sells you your morning paper. Fame is not necessarily an attribute of this person we're thinking about. What we're looking for is a person who has something, can do something, or exists in an environment which you'd like to experience.

The purpose of using *New Avatar Power* is to change your life. You need targets to aim at. Now, if the target is so different from your current way of life that you have trouble imagining what it's like to be at that pinnacle of delight, you need a symbol to pull you up by your bootstraps to reach that pinnacle.

The symbol for you is someone who has already done it. Your *Admiration Target* is that person, or those persons, who have achieved whatever it is you most desire at this time and place.

An extremely mundane example is one of desiring a luxurious new car. For some reason, you've never been to a showroom and sat behind the wheel of such a car. You think you have no hope in this life of owning such a magnificent vehicle.

You're wrong. All you need to do is plant a mental seed in the fertile soil of *New Avatar Power*, and that car is in your immediate future, as surely as if you had just given the salesman the cash for it and are now awaiting delivery of it.

The way to plant the seed is with your *Personal Verbal Seals,* and some of them are created directly from your *Admiration Targets.*

PERSONAL AVATAR VERBAL SEALS

To return to our example of obtaining a luxury car. Do you know anyone who owns one? Not necessarily a personal acquaintanceship: just his or her name is sufficient. You need never have seen the person: a photograph in the newspaper is sufficient, or even a news item saying, "Mr. XYZ is now the proud owner of Italy's latest auto creation: a V-12 de luxe version of the already superior Flamberrari Romano."

Mr. XYZ, for the purpose of getting your own car, is your *Admiration Target.*

VcToria Comments: Elon Musk came to mind as I was typing this in.

Or suppose you aspire to an overflowing bank account and all the trimmings which go with such wealth. You've often seen Lady Q. on television, doing the honors at ship launchings, flower shows, judging horses and the like. You know she's wallowing in the lap of luxury since her fourth husband settled enough money on her to make an oil baron turn green.

Lady Q. thus becomes your *Admiration Target* when you're creating *Personal Verbal Seals* designed to bring you everything you've ever desired in the way of luxurious living.

In less material vein, you may be seeking peace of mind and freedom from confusion and harassment.

Up in the hills lives a quiet and peaceful man. He seems to be poor, rarely appears around town, and is never seen whooping it up at parties.
You may have thought: "I wish I had his calmness and philosophy."

So have *New Avatar Power* bring you his peace of mind. He becomes your *Admiration Target*; no matter if his name is unknown to you. Give him a name, in your mind. Mr. Peaceful, Mr. Hermit, Fred Bloggs—not im-

86

portant, as long as *you* know whom you're thinking about.

All you want is to emulate his peace of mind. You're not hankering after his life-style: you seek more than a shack in the hills and raw carrots for breakfast.

VcToria Comments: After thinking about the 'peaceful' comments here, I realized that after many decades of profound shifting, with a ton of help from Dad's books, and my own intentions to allow change, I have created this feeling. I wrote a 'memoir' **Then Now and Forever** by VcToria Gray-Cobb [revised in 2020], that shows the journey I created in my twenties, and how in my forties I realized that I had to 'sink or swim'. Luckily I chose to 'swim'. Available on my website and Amazon.

Having acquired Mr. Peaceful's calmness, you can proceed to acquire Mrs. Q.'s millions and luxury. *New Avatar Power* is very happy to mix-and-match for you until your life is exactly the way you want it to be.

In brief, when you're reaching out with *New Avatar Power Secrets* to have something brought to you, and you wish to sharpen up the process, you acquire an *Admiration Target,* using the name [or an invented one] of a person who has what you desire.

EIGHTH SECRET OF NEW AVATAR POWER: CREATING YOUR PERSONAL VERBAL SEALS

Here we go into the process of creating the most powerful personal phrases you've ever used. Truly keyed to your personality and inner self, they represent the faucets, pipes, and nozzles which will direct the stream of *New Avatar Power* to work your miracles.

The language to be used is your own. If you feel more comfortable talking in Spanish, Italian, French,

PERSONAL AVATAR VERBAL SEALS

Serbo-Croat or any language other than American English, create your *Personal Verbal Seals* from that language. If you talk with a Deep South accent, that's part of your *Seals*, making them unique to you. Perhaps your grandmother was Scottish and you've retained some of the characteristic accent; then that gets knitted into your *Seals*.

They come from within you, in a form which you create. You make them in two forms, for two different kinds of purposes.

For both, you use the name and initial you're applying to yourself in your *Confidential Corporeal Commands*.

A complete *Personal Verbal Seal* goes together as simply as this: I (*name, initial*), wish to emulate (*name of Admiration Target*) in respect to (*announce what you wish to obtain, or what you wish to become*)."

Use your words, provided they mean much the same thing. "Wish to emulate" can become "desire to be like" or "aspire to be the same as." But please keep one English word out of your *Seal*: that word is "want." Do *not* say: "I, Rick W. want to be like Elon Musk....". Perhaps because of its close resemblance to the *Mysterious N'T Words*, "Want" is a forbidden word—I've found it impedes *New Avatar Power* when used within a *Seal*. (Why? Frankly, I'm still trying to find out—when I do, I'll publicize it in my next book.)

Change "in respect to" if that's not a phrase you would use. Use "acquiring" and adding "like his" (or hers) after you've stated your aim.

Another example: "I, Rick W., wish to be like Elon Musk, acquiring poise and success like his."
Get the picture? You tie your personal identity to your *Admiration Target,* telling *New Avatar Power* to have a similar asset transferred to you.

The second type of Personal Verbal Seal needs no *Admiration Target*. At least, not a person. This second

PERSONAL AVATAR VERBAL SEALS

type is used when you know exactly where you need to aim and are confident you know how it feels to be there.

Very simple. This *Personal Verbal Seal* is short and to the point. Having identified what you desire, you state: "I, (*Name, initial*), desire to (*mention your desired result*)."

Once again, use what word you please in place of "desire." "Wish," "aspire," "have set my heart on," "require"...anything which means the same, *except* of course the prohibited *Almost*-N'T *Word* "want": keep that one out of your *Seals* at all costs.

Of course, the desired result is simple: "Have money to pay this pile of bills"; "find a perfect lover"; "bring glowing health to me," —those are the kinds of things you request.

Notice the application of the *First New Avatar Power Secret*: it's easier to bring things to you than to send things away, so gear your desired result to that thought.

And, for you dippers and skippers, please note you can create a *Personal Verbal Seal* and shout it from the highest mountain or until your larynx goes rusty, and it's unlikely to have any effect.

As I'm about to explain, *Personal Verbal Seals* are used under special conditions to guide and channel your *New Avatar Power* in the correct directions.

HOW TO USE YOUR PERSONAL VERBAL SEALS

This brief section ties much of what has gone before into a neat blue-ribbon package. It sets up a sequence of events which ultimately culminates in personal miracles for you. I shall be referring back to this process, telling you to *Apply Your Verbal Seal*. When you come across that phrase, you'll know it means you

89

PERSONAL AVATAR VERBAL SEALS

carry out the step-by-step process I'm about to describe.

Little new to master here. You've already practiced almost every step.

First, recite your *Confidential Corporeal Commands.* Next, pretend your board or screen is in front of you. Then, in a neat game of make-believe which will assuredly become reality, mentally put a picture on your screen of your *Admiration Target,* or of *you* in the situation you desire, if you're using the second type of *Personal Verbal Seal.* As you do this simple piece of mind work, run your *Personal Verbal Seal* through your mind. Say it aloud if you wish, *but only if you're certain no one will hear you.*

You've done it. Your desire is impressed on your *New Avatar Power* stream. Easily and without fuss, your desire is being created for you, ready to envelope you in a cloud of happiness and delight. Open your eyes and carry on with whatever needs doing.

EVERYTHING YOU'VE LEARNED SO FAR KNITS INTO A PERFECT LIFE-CHANGING PACKAGE

Another quick summary of the progress so far will show you how the *Secrets of New Avatar Power* go together into a logical and powerful form.

One time only (although you can repeat the process any time you wish) you have heard and seen *Cosmic Energy* around you. You have identified your problems in your *Mystic Initiation* list. Of course, as they are miraculously solved, you will cross them off your list, and (if necessary) add any new ones. About once a month, you should rearrange your *Mystic Initiation* list, deleting problems which have vanished into limbo, and inserting anything new which has shown up (or which you forgot before). Additions or changes to the list are inserted in the appropriate place, renumbering the list as necessary. Use the same priority identifying technique as you used the first time.

Desired solutions will change. For example, the single-car garage may need updating to a three-car service bay, when you decide one luxury car is insufficient for your new life-style. So while you're rearranging the list of problems, change the desired solutions to match.

Your *Confidential Corporeal Commands* are now a regular part of your thinking patterns and the *Mysterious N'T Words* are appearing less and less in your life as you eradicate them. You're using the *Superb Uncertainty Banisher* whenever you have a difficult decision to make. Your enemies are becoming less and less harassing as you put up your *Seventh New Avatar Power Secret* defenses.

You have a collection of *Personal Verbal Seals* keyed to your various needs you're working on, and you're applying them as and when you wish. A daily *New Avatar Power* workout is fine, especially if you can do it at the same time and place. But if that's impossible, fit the work between your regular daily tasks as convenient.

YOU'LL BE AMAZED TO COMPARE YOUR FUTURE WITH YOUR PAST

One more thing needs doing before we look at more *Secrets of New Avatar Power*. Memory is often short and fallible, so you need to make, in the here and now, a brief record of the conditions of your life.

Then, in a month, two months, a year, you can look back and compare the startling changes which have taken place and see the path *New Avatar Power* is taking you along toward total fulfillment and automatic dream satisfaction.

You did most of the work when you put together your *Mystic Initiation* problem list. Take a look at that

PERSONAL AVATAR VERBAL SEALS

list and, just as if you were writing a diary, briefly summarize what's wrong with your life, and what you wish to see happen to make things easier and happier. Date the record and put it away for a full month.

Before re-reading this stored record, write out another summary of where your life has gone in the ensuing four weeks. Then compare the two records, putting them both away together for a month, when you do it again.

Again, there's no need to write a whole book. A few words on each problem and the solution you see as desirable are sufficient. One area to take especial note: when a problem has been solved, note how *you* figured it might be done, and note how *New Avatar Power* overcame it.

Thus you can chart the path *New Avatar Power* is taking you along—and it can read like an exciting novel.

SUMMARY OF CHAPTER 4

1. This chapter ties all planes of experience into a logical and powerful whole
2. Decide on your *Admiration Targets* to create your *Personal Verbal Seals.*
3. The word "Want" is a forbidden word when creating *Personal Verbal Seals.*
4. Make a brief monthly record of life conditions, and see the way you're going up to happiness.
5. Compare your solutions with the way *New Avatar Power* solves problems.
6. Just because this chapter has few items in its summary is no reason to believe it's less important than others!

Step By Step Miracles For You

5

STEP BY STEP MIRACLES FOR YOU

On we go together, uncovering two more *Secrets of New Avatar Power* and discovering the *Seven Negative Traps* and how to convert each one into the *Seven Desirable States*.

Having so far handed you the basic techniques of *New Avatar Power Secrets* (including eight of the *Secrets* themselves) we're now intent on sharpening your power to a fine edge which will lash through undesirable conditions and slay them as they stand, enabling happier conditions to grow.

STEP BY STEP MIRACLES FOR YOU

Although we've already covered a vast amount of ground, and your mind has been exercised in ways that you may not previously have known, I think you will agree that nothing we've covered so far is truly difficult. And the path is just as easy as we go on toward your perfect life.

LET NEW AVATAR POWER DO THE WORK

A small reminder is in order here. Following reciting your *Confidential Corporeal Commands*, you're in a physically relaxed and unwound state. Keep it that way when you're setting up any of the *Secrets*.

Some people have the idea that they must *force* things to happen by setting their jaw, gritting their teeth, clenching their fists, and generally tensing up like a bowstring.

That may be the way to win physical races, but all it will do to your *New Avatar Power* is have it seek a more relaxed channel to flow along.

Stay limp and unwound, allowing your mind to drift freely, setting up the pictures and thoughts directed. Willing things to happen, like an oldtime hypnotist, glaring, waving and forcing your willpower to operate is not the idea. You're shaping the flow of *Cosmic Energy* and that awesome force will do the work of shaping life the way you direct.

NINTH SECRET OF NEW AVATAR POWER: THE INCREDIBLE DISINTEREST REMOVER

Some aspects of this technique may amuse you, simply because you feel the thoughts I suggest are ludicrous. Smile if you wish, but please incorporate this *Secret* in your *New Avatar Power* routines. It does vital things to get your mind-moving as a chiropractor does to your bones when he manipulates your spine or a doctor does to your body when he gives you a medication.

As you're no doubt discovering, thinking is easy, but getting started on a mental path can often be a challenge, which is odd when you consider all you're doing is moving electrons along neural paths in your brain.

But if you've ever had to push a stalled car, you'll recognize a basic truth: the first shove has to be the biggest one. Scientists call this inertia: if something is at rest, it takes much greater effort to *start* it moving than it does to *keep* it moving once it starts rolling.

You may desire to start your mind thinking along a particular path, but find it idles happily, wandering in small circles, and willfully refusing to get started in the direction you want it to go.

Defeat this easily with the *Incredible Disinterest Remover.* Recite your *Confidential Corporeal Commands.* No need to pretend your screen or board is in front of you: this time we're going to go *inside* your head.

You know about the chunk of wrinkled gray matter inside your skull, called your brain. Think about the inside of your head, and pretend that instead of the gray matter, you have a skull filled with cold water. Your head is, if you like, a pan or kettle, sitting cold and stationary, on top of your spinal column.

Having got that idea firmly in mind, think about the base of your spine, down by your buttocks. For the purpose of this secret pretend your spine is not a series of interlocking vertebrae but a piece of piping with about a half-inch bore. You're going to pretend to send natural gas or butane up the tube to boil the kettle which is your head. (Well, I said this was a ludicrous technique—so it may seem, but you'll be amazed what it will do for your *New Avatar Power* work).

In your mind, pretend the gas is rising up your spine, inch by inch, and as it emerges at the top it pops into a searing hot flame which licks around the base of your skull, starting to warm the water we envisaged.

Small bubbles form in the water as the heat penetrates, and soon steam is forming, and the water reaches a full, rolling boil. Consider any pot on a stove you've seen doing this, and you've got the idea.

Tell yourself to "turn off" the gas, end this technique, and you're ready to proceed with your mind going a mile a minute. All mental blocks are cleared, and you can project your mind in any direction you desire.

A strange one indeed, but anytime you find your head feeling like a ball of cotton, without direction or motion, use the *Incredible Disinterest Remover* for instant brainpower.

TENTH SECRET OF NEW AVATAR POWER: THE STUPENDOUS POWER ENRICHER

This Secret does exactly what it says: gives you bursting, glowing mental energy which puts you ahead of your rivals in the game of life. The boost you get flows from you almost tangibly, enabling you to gain control over other people who previously defied you.

I'll be instructing you when to use this *Stupendous Power Enricher*. For the moment, carry out the technique, so you know how to do it.

Just as simple as all the rest, the preliminary work is identical to the *Incredible Disinterest Remover*. Go through that technique first until you've mentally got the water boiling furiously and you've turned off the gas.

All that steam can be used! Pretend that nature has given you a small pipe projecting from your brow, between your eyes and just above them. In your imagination allow the steam to rush out of that pipe in a thin white jet, under tremendous pressure, streaming out and forming a cloud which envelops whatever is in front of you.

Keep the stream going like a high-pressure jet for a few seconds, then open your eyes, dissolve the idea, and carry on with whatever you need to do.

That's the *Stupendous Power Enricher*. You'll understand how to make fantastic use of it as we incorporate it into situations described later.

THE SEVEN NEGATIVE TRAPS

Why are some people always happy and carefree, while others never seem to get lucky, never find life easy, and experience more sadness than they do happiness?

The answer is that the miserable people of this world have fallen into one or more of destiny's *Seven Negative Traps*.

When we've taken a brief glance at these snares of existence, you'll realize that *New Avatar Power Secrets* have a twofold purpose: first, to pull you out of these *Seven Negative Traps*, and second, to replace the conditions with the *Seven Desirable States*.

The Seven Negative Traps are:

1. *Fear*. Whether this is fear of a person or thing or an intangible fear of unknown conditions, we've already looked at how this corrosive emotion can keep happiness at bay.
2. *Uncertainty*. You're entitled to feel uneasy and upset if you're uncertain of your position. Change that to clear knowledge, and this trap loses its potency.
3. *Loneliness*. Humans crave companionship, and operate at less than their full potential without it.

Eradicate this vicious trap and life begins to brighten at once.

4. *Lack of Interest in Making Changes.* This is an insidious trap. Many people go through life under the influence of an attitude which says: "Better the devil I know than the one I do not." We've seen that to make life happier, changes *must* take place: that's the basic credo of *New Avatar Power*.
5. *Despair.* If fate has smitten you with catastrophes, indignities and frustrations, it's all too easy to metaphorically curl into a tight ball of despair and refuse to uncurl.
6. *Over-Sensitivity to the Influence of Others.* This is one of the most comprehensive traps of all. The dominating husband, the wide-eyed acceptance of false ideas, the concern about "What will the neighbors say?" are just three of the pitfalls which lead to this trap.
7. *Too Involved with the Troubles of Others.* This trap is all the more dangerous because of its two-edged standard. Agreed, we should be compassionate and helpful to those who are in trouble. But it's going too far to take on other people's troubles as if they were your own, worry about them, and use mental energy on something which is none of your business. Solve your *own* problems first, before trying to solve those of others is a fair guideline. Typically, the mother who lets her marriage fall apart because she constantly worries about whether her *son's* marriage is going to be satisfactory is well enmeshed in the coils of this trap.

THE SEVEN DESIRABLE STATES

The happy people on this earth have, by choice or chance entered into one or more of the *Seven Desirable*

STEP BY STEP MIRACLES FOR YOU

States. By eliminating the *Seven Negative Traps* and picking up on the *Desirable States* instead, your life becomes smooth and peaceful, ongoing and progressive, fulfilling and perfect.

Include in your *New Avatar Power* aiming points any or all of the following Seven Desirable States:

1. Good Luck
2. Power and Influence
3. Happiness
4. Love
5. Health
6. Use of Creativity
7. Wealth According to Needs

To perfect your existence, you do not necessarily have to achieve every one of the *Seven Desirable States*. In fact, some people are psychologically inharmonious if they get too much of No. 2. Others put No. 7 low on their priority lists. Maybe right now you feel that achieving No. 3 is all you seek.

So be it: but aim for one or more as you eradicate the *Seven Negative Traps* and you're aligned with the inner purpose of *New Avatar Power*.

YOUR MENTAL ACHIEVEMENT CHALKBOARD

This easy technique, which keeps your mind in the right framework to use *New Avatar Power*, requires you to pretend you have a chalkboard in front of you. It's a very simple method, and keeps you and your *New Avatar Power* up to date on how you're doing.

Recite your *Confidential Corporeal Commands* under the usual conditions, pretend you have a chalkboard in front of you and a piece of chalk in your hand. Now imagine you're writing up the names of any of the *Seven Negative Traps* you feel you're in at the time you're going through this exercise. Open your eyes and

103

use this book to remind you of their names, but close your eyes again before you pretend to do the writing on the board.

Once you've written them up, by name only, make a mental note of *how many* apply to you. Only how many—you need neither their names nor their numbers memorized.

In your mind, reach out with a duster and wipe them off. Now write the names of any of the *Seven Desirable States* you can honestly say you're rejoicing in at that moment.

Ask yourself which there are most of: *Traps* or *Desirable* States?

As you work with your *New Avatar Power* and carry out this *Mental Achievement Chalkboard* on, say, a monthly basis, you'll see the number of *Traps* growing less and the number of *Desirable States* growing greater.

Once you have an equal number of *Traps* and *States*, you know you're well on the way to happiness. When the States outnumber the *Traps*, life will be smooth. Finally, you find all the *Desirable States* you could wish for inscribed on your mental chalkboard and the number of *Negative Traps* you're in adds up to a big fat zero.

That's time for congratulations, because you'll then have clear evidence that you've beaten a malignant destiny and used your *New Avatar Power* to take you to the promised shining pinnacle of total fulfillment.

SUMMARY OF CHAPTER 5

1. The path is easy: let *New Avatar Power* do the work.
2. Stay relaxed when applying any *New Avatar Power* method.

3. The *Incredible Disinterest Remover* brings instant concentration and brainpower.
4. The *Stupendous Power Enricher* works at true magical and invisible levels, but its effects are tremendous.
5. When identified, the *Seven Negative Traps* are simple to escape from.
6. Aiming for any or all of the *Seven Desirable States* will bring peace and contentment into harassed lives.
7. Your *Mental Achievement Chalkboard* clearly identifies your *Traps* and *States* and enables you to keep score and move in the right direction for fulfillment.

Special Ways To Use The Secrets Of New Avatar Power

6

SPECIAL WAYS TO USE THE SECRETS OF NEW AVATAR POWER

Now you've got your basic *New Avatar Power* work behind you, we can look at some specialized ways of using it. The practice you've done with your *Confidential Corporeal Commands* and other *Secrets*, including the imaginary chalkboard or screen pretenses, were not simple gimmicks.

You've been shaping your thinking patterns so that you're now ready for what we can call *"Inner"* Se-

SPECIAL WAYS TO USE NEW AVATAR POWER

crets of New Avatar Power: ultra-powerful techniques which, if I had given them to you earlier, would have been less efficient because your psychic "muscles" had not been toned up.

SOME SITUATIONS NEED THE STRONGEST NEW AVATAR POWER TECHNIQUES

One occult fact you should always keep in mind: The longer a situation has been in existence, the more energy is needed to change it.

Thus, if you've been drifting deeper and deeper into debt and misery for 20 years, the situation is firmly "painted" into your environment, and it's going to take powerful applications of *New Avatar Power* to eradicate this stain on your happiness and peace.

I've watched *New Avatar Power* chipping away steadily at a situation, preparatory to blasting it away, thus taking a while to get the miracle performed. That depends on a whole load of factors, chief among which is how smooth or rough a channel you represent to *New Avatar Power*, which, of course, brings the responsibility back to you. Are you physically relaxed? Have you abandoned the *Mysterious N'T Words*? Are you following these suggestions the best you know how—all of the applicable ones, not just those which take your fancy?

Because if the answer to any of those last three queries is "No" then the *Eleventh* through *Twenty-First Secrets* should remain in your future until you've gotten the hang of the earlier ideas.

FATE SETS UP PART OF YOUR FUTURE FOR YOU TO WORK THROUGH

The *Thirteenth Secret of New Avatar Power* shows you how to know the future. With startling accuracy,

SPECIAL WAYS TO USE NEW AVATAR POWER

you're shown what's going to happen next, and you can thus guide your life more harmoniously.

But I'd like you to consider that concept for a moment. When we're looking at the future, what are we seeking? Obviously, pictures of events which exist someplace, maybe in a great Cosmic Blueprint, which are scheduled to occur.

Yet we're using *New Avatar Power* to *change* your life. So on the one hand we're looking at events which we find *will* happen, we're also setting out to alter your path into the future. Are those two viewpoints contradictory?

Not really, but the first does indicate one point which some people fail to recognize. No matter what "magic" you apply, *some* events will come your way. The script of the Universe has set things up that way, and for reasons which may not be obvious, your being, your soul, you as a person, are *destined* to live through certain episodes in your life.

When one of these inevitable events hits you, no matter how hard you apply *New Avatar Power* to try to divert it, use your *Secrets* in a different way. Stop wasting valuable energy in trying to escape: instead, use *New Avatar Power* to calmly sail through the fated situation instead of getting upset, worried, and harassed as you normally would by it. You can be sure, as I've said before, *New Avatar Power* is taking you toward a calm harbor of life where everything you've ever wanted is at your fingertips: but to get to that harbor by the quickest route, *New Avatar Power* may ask you to sail through a couple of storms to make the landfall!

ELEVENTH SECRET OF NEW AVATAR POWER: THE FANTASTIC LONELINESS ELIMINATOR

Now we're moving into the true *New Avatar Power* blockbusting *Secrets*. This one, and those which follow

SPECIAL WAYS TO USE NEW AVATAR POWER

may take a little more effort on your part, but the sparkling, fantastic results are true miracles. If you think you've seen some amazing results so far (and if you have not, you might wonder if your psychic muscles need some more workouts!) hold onto your hat!

Loneliness is, as we've noted, the third of the *Seven Negative Traps*. This corrosive state of mind needs attacking at physical, mental, emotional, and spiritual levels, because loneliness feeds on itself and requires powerful magic to unwind the skein and have you looking outward instead of inward. That magic is here, right now, with the *Fantastic Loneliness Eliminator*.

New Avatar Power will handle the inner work: the mental and spiritual areas of curing the condition. As your part of the equation, you have to apply a little *physical* involvement to complete the picture.

Arrange your personal schedule so that immediately following the mental work you can go out to a place where people are. Anywhere: a community center, a newsstand, a shopping mall, a library, a church. No matter if you know no one there—and if you're in the depths of loneliness that will likely be a fact.

Recite your *Confidential Corporeal Commands* as usual and mentally set up your screen or board. Now, within the frame of the square in front of you, pretend you're looking at a picture or a movie of people enjoying themselves. Any kind of fantasy you like: the key is that you're pretending to be viewing a happy, animated small crowd of people. Everyone knows everyone else, laughter is in the air, music plays (if you like music), and all the friendly and warm elements of life which you're missing in your loneliness are in your picture.

Now's the time to use a *Personal Verbal Seal*, put together as previously explained. The person who is part of the *Seal* has everything you hanker after. State

SPECIAL WAYS TO USE NEW AVATAR POWER

your *Personal Verbal Seal,* either firmly inside your mind, or aloud if no one is around to hear you.

Holding the picture in mind, open your eyes and go to the place I suggested. Stay for at least 15 minutes. Chat with anyone who hails you. More importantly, read any notices or leaflets which announce any event in your community which brings people together.

A public meeting, a lecture, anything where people are going to gather. No matter if the subject seems to be of little interest to you, make a note of the date and time, and arrange to attend. Try to make this an event which occurs within seven days from the present time.

On the day you're going on your *Fantastic Loneliness Eliminator* adventure, again perform the above *Confidential Corporeal Commands* routine, plus the *Personal Verbal Seal* and fantasy of observing people having a ball. Open your eyes, and off you go.

I'm guiding you no further along this fantastic path to togetherness: so many different things can happen to break your loneliness cycle. Be assured that condition is dissipating like sun warmed snow under the smashing impact of *New Avatar Power.*

TWELFTH SECRET OF NEW AVATAR POWER: THE STARTLING ASTRAL TRAVEL INDUCER

Many readers will know about *Astral Travel,* or *Astral Projection* as it's also called. It's a recognized state of mind and body where your awareness—the thinking, feeling, seeing, and hearing part of you—separates from your physical body and travels where you please.

Your body, deeply asleep, breathes, digests food, pumps blood, and does all the automatic things which it always does. But you have drifted away from it, un-

SPECIAL WAYS TO USE NEW AVATAR POWER

der full control, taking your abilities to see and hear what is going on anywhere in the Universe.

The possibilities of accomplishing miracles while *Astral Traveling* are limitless. You can uncover hidden facts, listen in on conversations, explore the world—explore other planets, if you wish—and zap instantly from one place to another like a wraith.

Rather than take up space which would fill the rest of this book and several others in explaining what *Astral Travel* is and what it can be used for, I'm going to give you the method. Once you've experienced this fantastic freedom of floating, flying, untouched by storm or circumstance, you'll open up to the astral realms and start to live!

Naturally, you need time to *Astral Travel*. Although you can zip from Los Angeles to New York in no seconds flat, you'll still spend time exploring while you're in either place. The incidents you view, the things you overhear, will take real time to experience, so applying this *Secret* requires that you can lie undisturbed for a while. Reckon on being "away" at least 30 minutes, at the minimum.

You *can* Astral Travel while your body is seated, but lying down is better. Your body needs to be comfortable, because physical disturbances will bring you back in a flash. I'll refer to that again in a moment.

Darken the room so that no bright lights shine in your eyes, loosen tight clothing, take off footwear. Do *not* put yourself into the same clothing which you wear to go to bed. If you do that, you'll merely drift off to sleep, and although you may *Astral Travel* in the sleep state, you'll probably not retain clear memories of where you've been, and you'll lose the tight control of destination which is a feature of true *Astral Travel*.

Lie down, and pretend your familiar movie screen or chalkboard is on the other side of the room. This time, make it a kingsize screen or board, about the size

SPECIAL WAYS TO USE NEW AVATAR POWER

of an average door, and imagine its lower edge is scant inches from the floor.

Now, get up and walk over to where you were pretending the screen was. Really get up, I mean; this piece of the technique is not all in your mind. Actually swing your legs off the bed or couch, stand up and walk across the room until you're standing in front of the space where your imagined screen was.

Now walk back to your chair, bed or couch and lie down, arranging yourself comfortably again. In your mind is a clear memory of the short walk you've just taken, across the room.

Recite your *Confidential Corporeal Commands*, slowly and carefully, attending to the inhaling and exhaling. When you reach the last "Relax," pretend your board or screen is back in place across the room.

In your mind this time, using your memory of having just done it, pretend you are standing up and going across the room to the screen. No problem in doing that: the memory of the actual walk you took is still crystal clear in your mind.

As you imagine you're approaching the screen, pretend it has turned into a door, which is open. Inside the door is someone you know and trust: anyone—a friend from long ago, a current lover, a revered parent.

Mentally reach out a hand *through* the door, and think where you would like to be. If it's a place where you've been before, call up a memory of the place. If it's somewhere new, just name and describe it in your mind, rather like a guidebook.

What happens next is a clear guide to what kind of a channel you've carved within yourself for *New Avatar Power*. Congratulate yourself heartily if zap! you're exactly where you said you desired to be. If you're still in your familiar room, go back to the top of the *Confidential Corporeal Commands* and give it a second try.

SPECIAL WAYS TO USE NEW AVATAR POWER

Still chained to the material plane? Third time lucky perhaps. Give it a go one more time.

If everything is in tune, you'll make it. If not, either you need more practice with earlier *New Avatar Power* techniques, or the time is not right. In either case, quiet your disappointment, and get up, going about your business in the normal way.

If you persevere with this, you assuredly *will* be able to *Astral Travel* and experience the amazing freedom I've described, and gain advantages.

BEST TIMES AND CONDITIONS FOR ASTRAL TRAVEL

Sometimes I believe more scary nonsense has been written about *Astral Travel* than about any other section of psychic or occult work, apart perhaps from possession and exorcism!

And even those last two frightening concepts have been grafted onto *Astral Travel*, which is as natural and carefree as going to sleep, and no more dangerous.

May I dispel a few myths?

Nobody has ever died while *Astral Traveling* because his soul was separated from his body and couldn't get back. That exists only in the pages of fiction and alleged true accounts of witchy goings on. Firstly, when you *Astral Travel* you do *not* ship your soul out of your body. Do that, and I agree you're in danger of being dead: soul-separating seems to be merely another description of death. It's really a matter of definition: *Paul Twitchell* practiced a discipline he called "Soul Travel," and his disciples maintain it's different from Astral Travel. They're entitled to their opinions: as far as I've been able to establish, Soul Travel is *Astral Travel* to special, spiritual destinations—an advanced form of the technique, but *Astral Travel* of a kind, for the body still functions perfectly while the soul is traveling.

Okay, no fears of death then. Separate from your body when *Astral Traveling*? You certainly are, but the early bother is not whether you're going to get cut off from your body, but much more strongly, whether you can stay "out" long enough to do whatever you've planned.

Understand, if your recumbent body is disturbed in any major way while you're *Astral Traveling*, you'll come back. Pow! In a nanosecond or quicker.

The telephone rings, someone yells "Fire!", a heavy truck vibrates your room, anyone calls your name, touches you, or if anything out of the ordinary which would wake you from the lightest doze occurs, you're back in your body, looking out of your physical eyes on your couch, and possibly vaguely resenting whoever or whatever recalled you so sharply from a splendid astral adventure.

A second half-truth connected with *Astral Travel* is that you meet dangerous and frightening demons while you're traveling, and they'll cause you harm.

Granted, something like that *can* happen, I kid you not, but the phantasms you're meeting are not horrible ghosts from the Pit. They're a clear sign you have not been working diligently enough on your *Fabulous Fear Eradicator*. Those ghoulies you think you're meeting are *your own fears*, dressed up especially by your own subconscious to prevent you experiencing the manifest joys of *Astral Travel*.

These self-generated phantoms *cannot* harm you, and the simplest way to "exorcise" them is to cut short your astral trip, work some more on your *Fabulous Fear Eradicator*, and then try the astral journey again.

How do you come back from an Astral Journey? Simple. You merely say to yourself *Return* and think about your room where your body is lying. Bingo! You're back.

One more myth to destroy. According to some writers who seem to enjoy trying to scare people, when you come back you can find another soul has taken over your body, leaving you to stroll in limbo for eternity. There are immutable Occult Laws which prevent that kind of malarkey occurring.

Enjoy your Astral Journeys. Be peaceful, and consider some very metaphysical words of the late Franklin D. Roosevelt. He might almost have been talking about *Astral Travel*, when in his First Inaugural Address almost half a century ago, he said: "Let me assert my firm belief that the only thing we have to fear is fear itself."

GET AHEAD BY KNOWING WHAT'S GOING TO HAPPEN

If you think about it, you'll realize we shape our lives by trying to second-guess the future. We call it planning, and spend long hours figuring the best way out of difficulties, the smoothest path into an unknown future.

When we guess right, that's fine. It's the *wrong* guesses, or our blindspots to unforeseen events which bring sticky problems.

"I wish I'd known then what I know now," is a sad cry you often hear when plans have gone awry or someone has missed a chance of getting some place good.

So what if there was a way to *know* what's coming tomorrow, instead of having to guess and hope you've guessed right? And not just tomorrow, but next week, next month, next year? A clearly unrolling movie of your future, to show you what's coming your way: then you'd streak ahead of the opposition.

SPECIAL WAYS TO USE NEW AVATAR POWER

It's here: *The Magic Future Knowing Technique* is offered for your assistance toward the brighter future you so richly deserve.

THIRTEENTH SECRET OF NEW AVATAR POWER: THE MAGIC FUTURE-KNOWING TECHNIQUE

You could consider this *New Avatar Power* method as the most effortless and automatic of all, even though it's one of the most fantastic, powerful, and life-changing of all of them.

Effortless because this one goes on automatically while you sleep, and all you have to do is make a note of what's revealed to you.

Before you retire for the night, put a pencil and pad beside your bed. If you have heavy drapes, or you habitually wake while it's still dark, you'll also require a bedside light.

The *Magic Future-Knowing Technique* starts just before you drift off to sleep. Begin as you're beginning to drift into the pre-sleep detached state, where you're warm, comfortable, and tucked down waiting for Morpheus to overtake you.

Recite your *Confidential Corporeal Commands*. Then pretend your usual screen or board is standing where you could see it if you opened your eyes. Pretend some kind person has pinned a calendar onto your screen. Begin counting up from 1, slowly and regularly, in your mind. As you name each number, pretend that the pages of the calendar are drifting off the board, floating down to make a pile on the floor.

If you reach 365, stop, and go to sleep. If, as is more likely, you drift off to sleep before you reach 365, that's even better.

You've attuned your inner mind and *New Avatar Power* to have you dream a dream *which is important to your future path.*

SPECIAL WAYS TO USE NEW AVATAR POWER

When you wake, grab the first thought which is in your head. "What was I thinking as I came to consciousness?" is the decisive question. This will bring any dreams to the surface for recall.

Do not wait until you've washed and dressed, believing that the clear and vivid dream you've woken with will stay. Nine times out of ten, a few minutes after you wake all you'll be left with is a memory that you dreamed something important.

Before you do anything else, write down any dreams you can recall. Notes are enough—no need to write a novel. But highlights to keep the memory from slipping; especially, make notes of names, numbers and dates which were in your dream.

Keep these notes safely, along with the other *New Avatar Power* lists and records I've recommended you keep. You can be sure—provided you've also set up your *Mystic Initiation* list, and gone through the preceding exercises—that your dream shows you how to solve a problem, or brings something to you which you need.

The importance of paying attention and acting on the information received is from *New Avatar Power* and it will gladly give you facts, but you have to go ahead and act on them.

VcToria Comments: I find a great degree of people do not follow through on messages that they have asked for, and therefore seem to waste the Universal energy that goes to great lengths to communicate the path needed to take.

As you know I have removed all of the original testimonials, but I am going to add one of my experiences here for you all to read.

In my psychic reads to clients I often meet old souls. This is interpreted from the Numerology charts that I erect for them. About 18 years ago a lovely young lady came to me for a reading. She was 21, highly at-

SPECIAL WAYS TO USE NEW AVATAR POWER

tractive, and at the time a personal trainer at the downtown gym. I explained to her that her chart indicated she was an old soul [a Life Path 22] and said to her 'here is the way to determine what you are here to do with your life' I gave her similar instructions to my Dad's, but used 'make a letter and put it under your pillow'. She did so, and the following week returned to me excited to explain to me what had happened.

"In my dream she said, a hand came out of a cloud with a basket. I knew I had to put my hand in the basket, so I did. I pulled out a piece of paper and on it were the words 'be a herbalist'. Then I woke up".

She continued to tell me that she headed to the gym and had a new client that day. Now I will never forget what she said to me next. "Normally my new clients just reach out and shake my hand as they introduce themselves, but not this one. She handed me her business card, and as I looked at it I was astounded. It read 'herbalist teacher'". She grinned at me.

Now I would love to tell you all that this lively 21 year old quit her job and followed her 'shown path' but she did not. Six months later she came for a read and was still working as a personal trainer enjoying all the boys who dated her etc. etc.

I never saw her again and always wonder if she ever followed her true path. Who knows, maybe she will read this book and recognize herself and get in touch. The Universe works in strange ways.

This though, is an example of wasting the energy of the Universe who clearly spoke when she asked.

FREEWILL IS OF GREAT IMPORTANCE

Whoever created this Universe we exist within gave us all a priceless gift, to use or misuse as we wish.

That gift is *free will*: the ability to decide to do something, or not to do it. Free will is part of your life-

SPECIAL WAYS TO USE NEW AVATAR POWER

changing *New Avatar Power* methods. We've seen in the previous case history that I, VcToria, wrote about how free will is used.

So what's the solution? Act or don't act on information received through *New Avatar Power*? My advice is to follow up on anything which *New Avatar Power* hands you: if it comes from a *New Avatar Power* technique then, by definition, it's designed to lead you towards happiness.

SUMMARY OF CHAPTER 6

1. Previous chapters, while extremely useful in their own right, were also getting you ready for the *Inner Secrets* from this chapter onward.
2. The longer a situation has existed, the more energy is needed to change it.
3. *New Avatar Power* works instantaneously at times.
4. Some events are pre-ordained. Use *New Avatar Power* to make the best of the inevitable.
5. The *Fantastic Loneliness Eliminator* lives up to its name!
6. *Astral Travel* offers endless opportunities to acquire knowledge and benefits.
7. Many false stories circulate about *Astral Travel*, alleging it to be dangerous. None of them stand up to investigation.
8. Knowing the future is a simple way to smooth your path and find profit.
9. The *Magic Future-Knowing Technique* is effortless and automatic.
10. Free will is destiny's gift to you. *Use* the data *New Avatar Power* brings you, do not ignore it.

Secrets Of Total Happiness Through New Avatar Power Techniques

7

SECRETS OF TOTAL HAPPINESS THROUGH NEW AVATAR POWER TECHNIQUES

VcToria Comments: I left the opening paragraph to this chapter as it pertains to where we will go in activating happiness.

"All I want is to be truly happy," said Liz S. in a recent letter. *A* splendid ambition, and one which *New Avatar Power is* designed to bring you. But when I

SECRETS OF TOTAL HAPPINESS

asked Liz what she needed to reach that desired state she answered: "I don't know. Like, I've never known what happiness is. I just want to be happy, that's all."

Her letter is one of the reasons this book was written. In order to use *New Avatar Power* to achieve any ambition, it needs the "launching point," the aiming point we discussed in Chapter 1. Liz found happiness coming but slowly because she had only a woolly idea of where she wanted to go and what she required for happiness.

VcToria Comments: I have addressed this feeling many times in person to my clients, and also on my Face Book videos. You cannot attract anything before you have 'inner peace'. That, in my opinion is 'happiness'.

Obviously, happiness means different things to different people. For some, a bag of gold would, they know, bring total happiness. Another person will say "The heck with lots of money: get me out of this monotonous job"; a third person is seeking merely a quiet place to meditate in the hills, with enough supplies to provide basic necessities; a fourth person sees being a play-person, with cars, planes, mansions, parties, and high living as the pinnacle of happiness. The list is as varied as the people we ask.

You need to know what kind of happiness you seek. Because when you know for sure, then your *New Avatar Power* can latch onto your ideas and create it for you.

Worry not about making the wrong choice. You may decide a luxurious penthouse is for you, and having reached it, find you're discontent with the surroundings, or the neighbors parties keep you awake, or a thousand-and-one things you failed to foresee make you less than transcendentally happy.

Never mind. It's a step in the right direction. Modify your plans, and let *New Avatar Power* take you the next step of the way. You'll end up happy, assuredly, and on the way you'll find out a great deal about your own likes and dislikes which will serve you well in maintaining that happiness.

YOUR TOTAL HAPPINESS LIST

"Another list? Could we not just make *mental* notes? I seem to have a dozen lists of varying things lying around. Are they of any use to *New Avatar Power*?" Without question. They're all part of providing aiming points for *New Avatar Power*. Writing a list does one very important thing: it forces you to focus your mind on the subject at hand. The very act of writing the words puts the thoughts into order where *New Avatar Power* can "read" and act on them.

When we merely think something, it's hedged around with all manner of sidetracks. Writing things down removes the obscuring mental foliage, and lets us see the facts.

Find time, along with your other approximately monthly *New Avatar Power* reviews of circumstances we've looked at, to fish out your *Mystic Initiation* list and any other relevant notes you've made.

Spend a delicious few minutes toying with the thought of future total happiness. Then get your pencil working and make *Your Total Happiness List.*

In capsule form, tell yourself what conditions you envisage which will make you finally, totally and utterly content with your life. What will be around you? Who will be beside you? What will you do with your days? What is your utmost, tip-top fantasy of life as you wish it to be?

Write the date on your list and put it with the rest of your *New Avatar Power* records. About once every month scan through it, and make any amendments which fit your latest state of mind. Of course, when any circumstance you've listed becomes sparkling reality, you can delete it from the list.

Yet I'll lay a quiet Astral wager with you that your list will never grow short—new items of delight will be forever popping in to keep it going!

FOURTEENTH SECRET OF NEW AVATAR POWER: THE MIRACULOUS DESPAIR DEFLECTOR

No matter how fortunate we are, times occur when the world looks less positive than usual. "It's just not my day," say some. "Got out of the wrong side of the bed," say others. Despite our strongest efforts, destiny is frowning.

To give you the reasons would require a long journey into metaphysics, and along the way we'd need to look at numerology, psychology, karma, reincarnation, astrology—a whole vista of occult, psychic, and scientific subjects which are beyond the scope of this book. To make *New Avatar Power* work, there's no need to take that trip.

So accept what you know to be a fact: some days are better than others. If you can accept that philosophically, fine. But some people interpret these less-than-good times as the end of their world, ultimate catastrophes, and retire into a sad state of despair.

Listen carefully: that's undesirable. Enjoy your misery, if that's what you need right then, but notice what you can be doing to your destiny path.

New Avatar Power, now pitching for you at all levels, stimulated by your application of preceding *Secrets*, is busy bringing your desires into reality. If you sit around moping, expecting the worst, visualizing life as a series of insoluble problems, setbacks and frustrations, it's just possible that New Avatar Power can pick

SECRETS OF TOTAL HAPPINESS

up your black thoughts and determine, because you're clinging so firmly to such dire ideas, that's what you're desiring to happen.

Unlikely, if you've done the basic work properly and set up happiness targets, yet some people are psychologically set so they drift into deep valleys of despair at times, and those mental images can overcome the positive pictures they've been painting,

Thus, instead of happiness coming along, *New Avatar Power* faithfully picks up on your new concepts and brings them to pass.

As I said, this is an unlikely condition, but having seen it occur a few times, I must include this warning, plus—more importantly—a weapon to prevent such unpleasant results.

Your weapon is *The Miraculous Despair Deflector.* Anytime you're feeling really "down," in a Cosmic Pit of Despair, when (as Dion Fortune so delightfully expressed it) "the skies are of brass," nothing is going right and you think you've been born under an evil star, three applications of this technique will dispel the conditions with a certainty and magic you'll find totally restful, relieving, and beautiful. More importantly, perhaps, you'll be erasing mental concepts which could have *New Avatar Power* taking you on an unintended course.

This is one of the few *Secrets* which have a "When" attached to them. For most potent effects, you need to carry out this technique at specific times—or at least, on particular days.

This takes a visit to your library, a call to your local newspaper, planetarium, or a peek at an almanac, because the *Miraculous Despair Deflector* is keyed to the phases of the Moon.

VcToria Comments: With the world wide web [www] now here, you only have to Google anything. I also give the Moon times in my monthly newsletter that can be printed out.

See my website www.alternativeuniverse.ca and sign up for the newsletter.

You're going to set up three dates to work this technique, spaced nine days apart. What day is the New Moon, in any month? That's one key date. The other two are 9 days *before* New Moon, and 9 days *after* New Moon. Thus, every month, three (occasionally four) days occur when this technique is favorable. If you're a person who regularly drops into moods of despair, it's worth your while to get an almanac for the year and mark the dates on a calendar, so that when you wake up with one of your black moods coming on, you can glance at the calendar and note the next favorable date for applying the *Fourteenth Secret*.

If you're totally unable to work this technique on a favorable day, the day before or the day after the marked date is almost as effective.

On the first favorable day, recite your *Confidential Corporeal Commands* as usual. On your familiar board or screen, pretend there are pictures of your forebodings, the things which are causing this mood of despair. If you're merely weighed down under an invisible cloud of negativity, and can't put your finger on the source, imagine a big, black query mark is floating on your screen.

Blank the screen and erase the picture, by whatever method you've been using before. Now "see" the same picture you used at the end of the *Third Secret: The Extraordinary Happiness Restorer*. End this session in the same way. Repeat this on the next two favorable dates.

SECRETS OF TOTAL HAPPINESS

BANISH BAD AND REPLACE IT WITH GOOD

Have you recognized the pattern of what we're doing with *New Avatar Power*? What we're doing, very simply stated, is to banish what you feel to be "bad," and replacing it with "good."

The brief point I'm making is that it's all very fine to banish the bad, and many occult and psychic methods recommend that. But that creates a kind of vacuum: having banished the bad things, you must replace them with something else, or they'll come creeping back again.

So having cleaned up the undesirable, we fill the gaps we've made with desirable things. As simple as that, but vital.

FIFTEENTH SECRET OF NEW AVATAR POWER: THE SPONTANEOUS HEALTH REGENERATOR

Izaak Walton was right when he wrote: "Look to your health; a blessing that money cannot buy." All the perfumes of Arabia, all the most luxurious possessions, the most perfect surroundings are as nothing if you lack blooming health to enjoy life.

Here with a *New Avatar Power Secret* which has helped thousands, the technique is as old as the ills of mankind; use of it goes back beyond the limits of written history. The Ancient Healers of the Fertile Crescent made sure their patients used a version of this method to get well.

All I've done is to update it, and put it into a familiar framework for you, so that you can incorporate it with your *New Avatar Power* workings.

Using this *Secret* on a daily basis, whenever convenient, in conjunction with whatever medical treatment you feel inclined to apply, can truly work miracles of healing.

Please be advised of a fact which I have pondered long and hard over before reaching a decision. I am not going to include more than a passing mention of the fantastic cures which have figured for people who have incorporated this technique into their lives. The reason for this is because I wish you to be able to read this book!

That requires some explanation. Currently, here in Canada, and to a lesser extent in the United States, a strong groundswell of official displeasure is breaking over anyone who makes statements which are opposed to current scientific opinion in the medical field.

On Vancouver Island, not far from where I am writing this John H. Tobe, a dedicated and sincere believer in the benefits of natural foods, is suffering the full pressure of the law because one of his books stated that a certain diet would cure cataracts. Such is the official harassment that I am told he recently said. He may have to stop publishing his monthly Provoker, a magazine of health and natural diet. Because of his firmly stated ideas, and despite his producing people who have been helped by him, he is being severely harassed.

VcToria Comments: I have left Dad's comments, but they were written in 1978. Today we still have the harassment as people lean towards vegan and plant based. Health comes from natural foods that the body loves. As a vegan myself, I can only tell you that the transition from dead flesh, to foods that bring vitality, can only be experienced with 'trying' it. Foods that bring vitality are 'whole foods'. You can Google a vegan or plant-based lifestyle and decide yourself.

Now, if I start saying *The Spontaneous Health Rejuvenator* will *cure* your ills, I'm laying this book open to official censure. I'm not worried about myself: in this

SECRETS OF TOTAL HAPPINESS

field legal harassment is a bogey which comes to all unorthodox practitioners at one time or another. And *New Avatar Power* is very efficient at keeping such negativity at bay.

But what could happen is that this book could be impounded by authorities and banned. Thus, you'd never see it, which would be a pity. So I've reluctantly decided to avoid all cure case histories, to avoid the inclusion of one particular page making the whole book abhorrent to those whose sincere path, within the law as it stands, is to protect people from those whom they define as "quacks."

'Nuff said?

So if you're currently under the doctor, or taking any kind of treatment from a healer of any kind, use *The Spontaneous Health Rejuvenator* in conjunction with recommended health care and prescriptions.

As always, the technique is simple. On any night when you're not *Astral Traveling*, recite your *Confidential Corporeal Commands* as you begin to drift between waking and sleeping. Pretend your board or screen is before you, and on it appears a picture of you. But not the you who is sick or unwell: this picture shows you at a time when you were overflowing with health.

Think about your malady. Say you have varicose veins of the leg, lumpy, unsightly, and aching. In your let's-pretend picture, see your body as having smooth and strong limbs without a trace of the bulging and ugly veins. As you drift off to sleep, pretend your legs are as strong and healthy as you desire, smooth and unblemished.

Apply that technique to any malady: Put up a mental picture of you, changed to bursting vitality, with the disease completely eradicated, as if it had never been.

Allow yourself to drift off to sleep with that picture firmly in mind.

I leave you to work with this technique, without laying any claims which might collect negativity.

RESHAPING YOUR DREAMS TO BRING BENEFITS

We've looked at seeing the future as you lie dreaming, but there are other splendid benefits you can gain from the sleep state.

"It's only a dream," people say, suggesting dreams have no value beyond, perhaps, some slight entertainment.

Try poet *Percy Bysshe Shelley* instead. Now, he had the right idea about dreams:

It is our will
That thus enchains us to permitted ill—
We might be otherwise—we might be all
We dream of happy, high majestical."

Yes, you can help *New Avatar Power* along tremendously with a fascinating technique which takes up no time that you might wish to use otherwise. You do things with your dreams, purposely and under control, to help your life improve.

The basic knack is pretty simple to catch. Due to all these *New Avatar Power* exercises you're practicing, your mind will easily attune to what you're trying to do.

Next time you're asleep and realize you're dreaming, you become the "scriptwriter." Often in our dreams we simply watch the drama or events unfold while we observe or take part. A little known fact is that you can take full control of your dreams and steer them where you wish at times. Not *all* of the time: dreams are important safety valves for your inner mind, so sometimes a dream will steam ahead on its own course, and there's nothing you can do about it. Also, if you're getting a future picture shown to you, your best efforts to alter the dream will come to naught.

But often you *can* alter the dream. Try it in small ways at first, such as dressing yourself (in your dream) in the finest outfit you can imagine. Then sketch in other desirable details: bring yourself a perfect lover, if that's what you need. In fact, move the "plot" of your dream around so you're fulfilling anything which is on your *Total Happiness List.*

Also reinforce your *Spontaneous Health Rejuvenator* by ensuring that your dream self is healthy and fit.

Such sleep games do fantastic back-up work for *New Avatar Power* by putting the right ideas in exactly the right place: deep in your mind where *New Avatar Power* is strongest.

HOW TO INVADE THE SLEEPING MINDS OF OTHERS

While on the subject of dreams, did you know you can influence others by altering *their* dreams? This technique is a true piece of Magic, used by wizards and occult practitioners for centuries.

Having mastered the knack of *Astral Travel,* you'll find you can easily walk into anyone's bedroom while they're sleeping. Your *Astral Self* will be able to talk to the person concerned.

To influence someone in this manner, *Astral Travel* to their home at a time when you believe they'll be asleep. If you find them whooping it up at a late-night party, that's too bad—come back some other time.

Only if your contact is deeply asleep will this work properly. Walk to the sleeper (and you're doing this in the *Astral* state, remember, so no one's going to wake up and arrest you as a burglar!). Lay your hands on the sleeper's brow and state your requirements.

SECRETS OF TOTAL HAPPINESS

If it's your bank manager who's snoring peacefully before you, your statement is: "You *will* grant me the loan I requested yesterday."

If it's a desired lover who refuses to recognize you exist, you state: "Next time you see me you will respond to my approaches. I am in your dreams and you see me as a perfect, compatible partner."

That kind of long-distance influence, which is a kind of *Astral* hypnotism, can have fantastic effects for you.

SIXTEENTH SECRET OF NEW AVATAR POWER: CHARGING YOUR AURA WITH COSMIC ENERGY

Just as a car works more efficiently and starts more promptly when its battery is fully charged, so can you find instant effects for yourself by charging your own powerplant.

Your central driving force, your soul, or whatever else you like to call it, radiates a force-field around you, just as an electric motor has a magnetic field around it when it's working.

Depending on your state of health and vitality, so your personal force-field grows larger or smaller. The name, which you may have heard for your force-field, is "aura." Some sensitive people can see it, surrounding your physical body in a shimmering sphere of energy, extending up to three feet or more from your body.

Many day-to-day encounters stand or fall, depending on how strongly-charged your aura is. When you stand close to a person, your separate auras intertwine. They may reinforce each other, and you feel a mutual bond of friendship and co-operation; they may fail to mix, in which case little happens between the two of you; or they may repel each other, in which case the pair of you hate each other on sight.

Whichever happens, the aura which is most strongly charged belongs to the person who gains most from whatever exchange is going on, whether it's wheeling and dealing for a car, or making someone do you a favor, ranging from lending you ten dollars to eloping with you!

Thus, a fully-charged aura helps you in life's battles. Here's how to charge up your Aura to a million psychic volts, and eclipse every aura which comes near yours for the next 24 hours.

Carry this out in private: you need to wave your arms about, and although you might tell the inquisitive that you're practicing calisthenics or Yoga, the better solution is not to attract attention.

Stand up where you can stretch your hands and arms out all around you without banging your knuckles on walls or furniture. Recite your *Confidential Corporeal Commands* keeping your eyes closed after reaching the final "Relax," put your arms out level in front of you exactly like a diver who is about to plunge off a diving board.

Slowly sweep your arms out to the sides, so you're standing like a letter "T." Now move your arms up until your palms are together above your head, arms as straight as possible.

Move your hands back, lift your chin, inhale and arch your back as much as you can. Begin to breathe out, straighten up, and bring your hands down to the "T" position.

Bring your hands slowly down to your sides. Take three deep breaths after your hands reach your sides.

You're fully charged with Cosmic Energy.

VcToria Comments: About 20 years ago, I was with three of my grandchildren at an Earth Day celebration in Hawrelak Park in Edmonton, Alberta, Canada. They were playing a game called 'Shark' with a volunteer while I sat on a picnic bench and watched from about ten feet away. I had my head resting in my hand, and my elbow on the table. I was day dreaming and my mind went blank for one second.

All of a sudden the volunteer's aura appeared to me. A brilliant pink and white, about one foot in diameter all around her head. Vivid and amazing. Colors that are much brighter than any here on the earthly plane. Now, one would think I would get up, maybe speak to her, touch the energy or even see if I could expand it? I did not. I think back to that day a thousand times, and wonder why I got bored looking at it and turned away for a second. I looked back and it was gone from my third eye/subconscious vision. I have never seen one again as vivid and strong as hers.

WHAT A CHARGED AURA CAN DO TO YOUR COLLEAGUES

No need to take my word for it when I say your Aura's fully charged. You can watch it in action and be amazed.

Anyone within three feet of you, even six feet on a good day, is under the domination of your vitalized Aura.
Try it on a friend. Move to within a few feet, and make a polite request which your friend might normally refuse.

Try the guy who's renowned for never lending a dime. Move in, Aura fully charged, and ask, "Could you lend me five dollars until payday, please?"

The instant response of digging deep into his pocket and pressing money on you—"maybe ten dollars would be better? Take it,"—can be the story of the month around your working area.

Or maybe you want a date. Approach the object of your desires and suggest a time, place, and event for

SECRETS OF TOTAL HAPPINESS

you two to have a pleasant time together. Cold and aloof ladies melt and agree. Snooty guys bow down and accept your suggestion with enthusiasm.

Amazing, but true—provided you use this in combination with your other *New Avatar Power* strengthening exercises. Just extracting this bit from the book without attending to the remainder of the exercises is futile; all you'll do is send me an "It Doesn't Work" letter.

SUMMARY OF CHAPTER 7

1. Define what kind of happiness you seek, thus giving *New Avatar Power* its vital aiming point.
2. When using *New Avatar Power*, no such thing as a "wrong choice" exists. You are taken step by glorious step to happiness, regardless of intervening incidents.
3. Your *Total Happiness List* brings your needs out into the open. Review the list monthly.
4. The *Miraculous Despair Deflector* prevents *New Avatar Power* from getting an incorrect slant on your ideas of what you most desire.
5. After banishing "bad" things, replace them with "good," so there's no space for the bad to come back. See also the *First Secret of New Avatar Power*.
6. Try the *Spontaneous Health Regenerator*. For reasons explained in the text, making claims for its efficiency is unwise.
7. Reshaping your dreams is a valuable *New Avatar Power* exercise.
8. You can influence others by invading their dreams.
9. Your central driving force benefits from recharging.
10. A fully-charged Aura can bring startling results.

Secrets of Wealth—
Incredible New Avatar
Money Activators

8

SECRETS OF WEALTH—
INCREDIBLE NEW AVATAR
MONEY ACTIVATORS

"Money is the root of all evil." Would you say that's a correct quote? Well, it's not: the actual words, from I Timothy, Chapter 6, Verse 10, are: "For the *love* of money is the root of all evil."

An important difference between the two statements. There's nothing wrong with money itself: but becoming obsessed with it to the exclusion of all else is

SECRETS OF WEALTH

not desirable. Remember that as we go through these steps to fabulous wealth for you.

WHERE ALL THE MONEY IS

Unlike *New Avatar Power*, where everyone has more than they need, money is spread unevenly through the world. A statistician once calculated that 20% of the people control 80% of the money. Putting that into figures we can understand more easily, it means that if you could select five people at random who had $100 in cash between them, one of those five would be most likely to be carrying $80, while the others would each have about $5 in their pockets—a disparity of 16 to 1.

That's a natural financial law which holds good everywhere: every fourth person you pass in the street is likely, on average, to be carrying 16 times more than you are—unless you've just robbed a bank!

So when you're moving from being in debt and permanently short of cash, you're jumping two hurdles: one which takes you from the 8-in-10 group of poorer people to the 2-in-10 group who control most of the available cash and assets; the second leaps you from one income bracket to another 16 times as large.

Thus when *New Avatar Power* takes you up in the world, the first step is a quantum leap: if you saw $6,000 pass through your hands last year, next year you're likely to see 16 times that amount—close to $100,000. You move from a majority to a privileged minority, and you'll find little in between: you'll notice *most* people are either poor or reasonably well off (but not wealthy) while the others are filthy rich, with so much money they spend their time paying people to figure out tax dodges for them.

Keep that 80-20 split in mind while you're working your *New Avatar Power* miracles: it puts the picture in perspective, enables you to see where you're aiming.

WHY YOU PROBABLY HAVE LESS THAN YOUR RIGHTFUL SHARE

Wealth is not just money in the bank. It's property, assets, valuables, plus intangibles like credit ratings, prospects, and influence, and power.

Each of those obey the 80-20 Law we looked at earlier: one person in five wields 16 times more power over his four nearest colleagues; one person can go into the bank and easily borrow $100,000, unsecured, while the next four average people have trouble raising $5,000 on their home as a fully-secured second mortgage.

You maybe own one house (or part of one, if you're still paying off the loan); you need to look only a short way before you trip over someone who is on the other pan of the 80-20 balance: he owns *sixteen* or more houses and collects rent from 15 of them while he luxuriates in the sixteenth.

Two things you can learn from these facts. First is that, with odds stacked up against you like that, it's hardly surprising you've got less than you need. And, much more happily, you'll know you're well on your way up the *New Avatar Power* path to incredible ease when you find you've got 16 times more than you had previously. You'll then know you're over the hump, and having made that leap, life gets easier by the day.

HOW TO ACQUIRE MONEY AND PROPERTY

The *First Secret of New Avatar Power* revealed that it's easier to bring things to you than to send things away. So acquiring, money and assets is exactly what the doctor ordered: in the most material manner, you do need to bring goods and cash to you in a golden stream to become wealthy. *New Avatar Power* is custom tailored to accomplish that small thing, and the *Eighteenth Secret: The Remarkable Money Renewer* hands you the method with pleasure in this chapter.

SEVENTEENTH SECRET OF NEW AVATAR POWER: THE PHENOMENAL OVER-SENSITIVITY TRANSFORMER

This *Secret* is inserted here with a purpose, just before telling you how to get filthy rich if you wish to. Right now you're under the influence of all kinds of people. Your boss tells you what to do and what not to do. Your financial adviser suggests you do this or that. More subtly, advertisers, in the papers and on TV, persuade you to part with money for various reasons. In obvious and less obvious ways, you're responding to the demands and pressures of an army of persuaders.

Once you're rich, the pressures become greater, not less. Get-rich-quick merchants present deceptively tempting schemes, swindles disguised as investments. Your relatives will descend on you in a bunch, telling you who deserves what and telling you how to spend your money. We could go on, but it would be a waste of valuable time.

What I'm suggesting is that before you make yourself wealthy, you totally overcome one of the *Seven Negative Traps* I told you about in Chapter 5.

That Trap is No. 6: *Over-Sensitivity to the Influence of Others*. Escape from that trap, and you're free to spend your money as you wish and let the crowds yammer outside. If they wish to spend money on such-and-so, tell them to get their own bucks together.

You do not need to be rich before you apply this *Secret*. Its effects and protection give you a masterful feeling of independence and freedom. You become your own person, make your own decisions. Yes, you listen to advice, but you no longer feel obliged to act on every input because you feel the other person may know something you may not know.

The *Phenomenal Over-Sensitivity Transformer* is the *Secret* I urge you to incorporate in your being today, with booster shots (doing it again) whenever you feel your control over your own life may be slipping and you're starting to take orders you dislike again.

Simplicity itself. Recite your *Confidential Corporeal Commands* and plant your screen or board in front of you. Having done this so many times before, you should almost feel if you reached out blindly, you'd actually *touch* it.

Mentally, put yourself on your screen. Alone. And naked. Consider who is the most commanding, powerful, in control person you've ever heard of or encountered. Male or female, no matter. A king, a queen, a dictator (someone whose policies you agree with), a chief, a boss, a leader of some kind.

Now, in your mind, see yourself wearing that leading person's clothes. No matter if you're the wrong sex to wear them, put them on your unclothed image in your picture.

Now pretend you, wearing your controlling clothes, climb up onto a stage, up three steps, turn around and sit in a comfortable chair, surveying anything or anyone who passes. Finally pretend a crew of workmen arrive, and at someone else's expense, build a box of clear bulletproof glass around you. The workmen bow, and depart.

In your mind, commandingly state the *Personal Verbal Seal* which fits this splendid occasion. The name you aspire to is, of course, the name of the person whose clothes you're pretending to wear.

There you sit. Up above interference, protected, and dressed as a commander. Leave the image on your screen as you open your eyes and carry on with whatever else needs doing.

EIGHTEENTH SECRET OF NEW AVATAR POWER: THE REMARKABLE MONEY RENEWER

Here's the Miracle you've been waiting for, right? One caution, please. Maybe two cautions. First be sure you've been practicing all other necessary *New Avatar Power* techniques. Second, recall the quote at the beginning of this chapter.

Here is where many people go adrift with *New Avatar Power*. Seeing promises of money, they ignore the rest of the book, hurriedly whip through the instructions here, and then wonder why a truck loaded with gold ingots fails to overturn in their yard.

So be it. If that's your trip, it *can* happen. Yes, I've seen people apply *New Avatar Power* and become millionaires inside three short days. By all means follow through and also become a millionaire, if that's what you truly desire. But if your main thought at this moment is, "If I had a million, I'd be truly happy" you may have your priorities upside down. More often than not, it happens the other way around: *"While I was becoming truly happy, I found I'd accumulated a million dollars."* The latter way is closer to how *New Avatar Power* works for the majority.

So you're in debt. How come? What put you in debt? Getting a cool million will solve immediate problems, but you'll still be the same person who got into debt. The original problems which got you in trouble in the first place may still exist. So getting the money will pay today's bills, but by tomorrow you can easily be back where you started, only in much deeper. Big money can mean even bigger debts!

SECRETS OF WEALTH

So spread your *New Avatar Power* efforts around a little. Solve the flaws which got you in your present unpleasant condition, simultaneously with bringing in the dollars. It's very hazardous to say, "First, I'll get the money and throw those collectors off my back. *Then* I'll get to other *New Avatar Power* work, without so many worries." That might work; but it might not. I've seen people acquire money, then get so involved in spending it and living it up that they postponed *New Avatar Power* efforts. "Next week I'll get to it," they said, and kept saying it all the way to the bankruptcy proceedings. Enough warnings? Just so you understand, that's all. Let's concentrate on money then, and good luck with your resulting fortune.

You guessed it: recite your *Confidential Corporeal Commands*. But before you do, have a dollar bill (or a five, a ten any piece of paper currency) within reach. Erect your imaginary screen or board. On your board pretend to write *the amount which is currently on your Mystic Initiation* list. Yes, that much, and not a dime extra.

That's exactly what your *Mystic Initiation* list is for: to show precisely what needs doing right now to solve your problems. And here we're solving money problems. Fair enough?

Later, when (and only when) you need it, you can write up your million dollars. But it *must* be money whose absence is truly a major inconvenience. Remember *New Avatar Power* brings you what you need to make you peaceful and fulfilled. If you're only $7,643 in debt, what's the balance of $992,357 for?

That's the line to take. Spell out the total you've already included on your *Mystic Initiation* list. Yes, I've said it before. I'd say it twenty times if I thought that would drive it home more firmly. It's *that* important.

So you've put the figure on your screen. Clean it off, switch it off, do whatever you've been doing before

151

SECRETS OF WEALTH

to erase things from your mental frame in these conditions.

Reach out, eyes closed, and pick up the currency I told you to have close to you at the outset. Put it beside your ear and rustle or crackle it with your fingers. Put it under your nose and inhale its odor. Hold it in front of your face, open your eyes and examine every square millimeter of the bill, on both sides. Absorb it into your mind. Put the bill back where you got it from, and close your eyes.

Pretend the bill is now pinned to your screen or board. The pin comes loose, and the bill falls to the floor, but you merely pretend it has been replaced with another one, maybe of a higher denomination (but only as large as you've personally handled). Tens and twenties are fine, but if you've never had your hands on a $10,000 bill, leave it out of the picture until one comes your way.

Continue to pretend the bills are drifting to the floor, making a growing pile which smells, sounds, and feels like the single bill you so recently experienced. When your screen is almost hidden by this welcome "money drift" of imaginary currency, mentally state a *Personal Verbal Seal* which fits this cash accumulation occasion, open your eyes and do whatever needs to be done next.

VcToria Comments: In regards to the above comments on the $10,000 bill. Yes, they existed. Both $5,000 and $10,000 bills were last printed in December 1945, but officially discontinued in 1969 for lack of use. They are still however, recognized as legal currency.

WHERE WILL THE MONEY COME FROM?

You've put *New Avatar Power* into action with the *Remarkable Money Renewer.* Your bills, installments, and other debts will be settled more quickly than you thought possible. But where will all that cash come from?

If you were anticipating a peal of heavenly bells and a trio of angels to come wafting through the window bearing gold, platinum, and diamonds, you're out of luck! The money will be made available in perfectly natural ways. As I and colleagues of mine have said before, if spooky things started happening with *New Avatar Power* and similar techniques, you'd not be heading for happiness, you'd merely collect a reputation for being a freak. Genies in bottles may be fine for TV comedies, but in real life they could be more a liability than an asset.

HOW TO MAINTAIN YOUR BANK BALANCE ONCE IT'S HEALTHY

If you feel it's a total necessity to have thousands of dollars lying unused in your bank account, go ahead and include them on your *Mystical Initiation* list. If such a lack is truly a problem to your happiness, be sure *New Avatar Power* will bring the necessary credit balance into being for you.

Entertain another thought. If each day, or each week, enough money came your way to meet your every need, that would be just as good as having thousands sitting on the ledger sheet of a bank which just *might* go belly up overnight, leaving you the wailing loser.

That's the way many experienced *New Avatar Power* users operate, and it brings great peace of mind. If you want to bring that close to home, I now operate that way, after years of considering a nest-egg was absolutely necessary. At any given moment I've got enough money in the bank to keep the account open and to meet immediate expenses. Then when I want something big I "tell" *New Avatar Power* and the money comes.

Example? I thought while I was working on this book that would be nice to give Marya, my wife, something fairly expensive for her birthday. Can't tell you what it is, because it's not her birthday yet, and she'll be reading this manuscript. She's my constant companion and helpmate, which is why she deserves an expensive gift.

That kind of money needed a boost from *New Avatar Power*. No more than four hours after a brief application of the *Remarkable Money Renewer,* my telephone rang.

It was a TV producer from Eastern Canada.
"Can you be in Winnipeg next month for a series of programs?" he asked.

That just happened (coincidence?) to fall into a gap in my normally crowded schedule. We bargained a while, and to cut the story short, I'm flying to stay at one of Winnipeg's finest hotels for three days next month, all expenses paid, to do about six hours on-screen TV work which is not only fun, it also pays a fee which matches the sum I was thinking I'd need. How much? Not telling, but I used to have to labor a full year to make that kind of money not too long ago.

That's the most peaceful way to use *New Avatar Power*. If you decide you need something, the wherewithal turns up right on the button, without fail, without fuss.

Consider that approach: I personally recommend it.

SUMMARY OF CHAPTER 8

1. Note the 80-20 split when you're looking at money matters.
2. Multiplying your assets by 16 shows you've made the quantum leap over the 80-20 barrier.
3. Remember the *First Secret of New Avatar Power* when you're accumulating money and property.
4. Armor yourself against manipulators *before* you get rich. The *Phenomenal Over-Sensitivity Transformer* can do it for you.
5. The *Remarkable Money Renewer* works—but please do not use it to the exclusion of all else.
6. Money will come in natural ways, even if coincidence plays a great part.
7. Consider whether you really need surplus cash locked up idle in the bank. A constant flow to keep well ahead of existing requirements is just as good.

Secrets Of Perfect Love, Romance And Marriage: How New Avatar Power Brings You The Love You Deserve

9

SECRETS OF PERFECT LOVE, ROMANCE AND MARRIAGE: HOW NEW AVATAR POWER BRINGS YOU THE LOVE YOU DESERVE

Sir Francis Bacon puts the theme of this chapter far better than I could hope to:

SECRETS OF PERFECT LOVE

"A crowd is not company, and faces are but a gallery of pictures, and talk but a tinkling cymbal, where there is no love."

YOU DESERVE LOVE AND ROMANCE: NEW AVATAR POWER WILL BRING IT

We humans, being made as we are, almost all of us need people. And within our circle of acquaintances and friends, we need *special* people. I'd call them lovers, if the word had not been so debased by popular literary usage. Yet the new word "cohab," short for cohabitator, still seems alien to me, and "companion" sounds somewhat like a paid retainer to a retired millionairess.

So I shall use the term "partner" to cover the multitude of relationships which love, marriage, companionship, cohabitation, affairs, crushes, passions, flirtation, and dalliance incorporate.

You know what love means to you, and that's the purpose of this chapter: to bring a partner to you who will fulfill, whether temporarily or permanently, your needs of this time.

Unless you are a most unusual person, you need love to function adequately, to be happy, to be fulfilled and content. Destiny wise, you deserve love to make you a complete and harmonious being.

So seek and ye shall find with the unfailing aid of *New Avatar Power*.

AIM HIGH WITH NEW AVATAR POWER

Now we're looking at an intangible—love—we can really open up to *New Avatar Power*'s stupendous ability to bring exactly the right conditions.

New Avatar Power is in its element when operating at relationship levels: much more goes on when you're with a partner than can be seen and measured by material means. We've briefly touched on the interaction of auras: that forms part of a love relationship, and with the right direction, *New Avatar Power* gladly manipulates conditions to match up to your highest expectations.

NINETEENTH SECRET OF NEW AVATAR POWER: THE EXCEPTIONAL LOVE ELEVATOR

Do you know whom you wish to attract? Is there someone in your circle whom you see as a perfect partner? Perhaps you already have a partner, but your relationship is not as vital and fulfilling as you would wish. Or maybe you're without a specific partner right now, and wish to see Mr. or Ms. Right come drifting into your orbit, to begin a relationship which makes Romeo and Juliet look uninteresting.

Whichever is your condition, the *Exceptional Love Elevator* changes all that. Bells ring, birds sing, and every last item which you comprehend by the phrase "Perfect Love" comes winging to you.

This *Secret* has greatest and most immediate effects if you perform it at Full Moon, but any other time will suffice.

Recite your *Confidential Corporeal Commands*. Erect your screen or board. If it's quiet enough, listen to your heartbeat, the traditional seat of love.
On the screen, I'd like you to pretend someone has drawn a large heartshape, in red crayon, lipstick or red paint.

Pretend the heart-shape is a window. You're looking through it at whoever is on the other side. If you already know who it is you wish to bind as a love partner, search in your memory for a mind picture of the last time you saw that person in the flesh. Replay the

SECRETS OF PERFECT LOVE

memory in your head, pretending the action is going on just to the other side of the heart on your screen.

If your partner is yet to be revealed to you, imagine that someone, anyone, is peeping back at you from the other side of the heart.

Now stand up and apply the *Sixteenth Secret, Charging Your Aura with Cosmic Energy,* explained in Chapter 7. No need to repeat the *Confidential Corporeal Commands*; you just did that a short while before.
That's it. The love wheels are in motion.

MAKING THE MOST EFFECTIVE USE OF THE EXCEPTIONAL LOVE ELEVATOR

As you end the *Aura Charging* you're radiating love magnetism at every level of your being and will continue to do so for 24 hours at high levels and about 14 days with lesser power. Recharge these love energies whenever you wish.

What next? Some action on the physical plane is best. Some while ago I had a letter from a young man who said he was desperately in love with a girl who lived 40 miles away. He'd met her briefly some five years before, she had never been introduced to him and presumably hardly remembered he existed. His request was that *New Avatar Power* make her call him by telephone and swear undying love to him. It's possible, but if you're beginning with *New Avatar Power,* it would be quicker to manipulate conditions somewhat.

Understand that working with *New Avatar Power* is unobtrusive and secret. Things come your way as if by coincidence or chance, always in reasonable ways. Take that girl the young man wanted to influence, for instance.

Consider how she would feel if she woke from a dream with an unknown long-distance telephone number in her head, and the image of someone who was her ideal before her. She *might* call that number and start something big going; but in the framework of her own impulses, she'd possibly dismiss it all as a dream, and if it persisted, go to her shrink and check it with him. Miracles, yes, but *reasonable* miracles, such that other people do not start looking at you as if you're a latterday Aleister Crowley or Svengali.

So give *New Avatar Power* maximum chances of working. Arrange your affairs so you *meet* the object of your desires. Be receptive, but *not* pushy. You're working at deep mind levels, forging delicate bonds. *Let the approach come from your potential partner.* Your magnetism will do the rest and create the love situation you most desire.

And if you have no one possible in mind, and the imaginary person in your *Secret* heart has yet to appear?

Circulate. Indeed, it's true *New Avatar Power* can bring your ideal love tapping on your door. But you're opening up to quicker and wider opportunities if you get out into the outside world where you meet people. Any people: among them is your unknown love target.

Can you do anything else? Sure you can. If your future partner is unknown to you, go *Astral Traveling* whenever convenient. The people you meet on the *Astral Plane* frequently appear in the flesh, later, and you've taken a very important bonding step if you've already met your partner astrally, before the partnership becomes a physical reality in the here and now.

You have even more powerful weapons of attraction when you clearly know your desired partner. Remember Chapter 7 and walking into the sleeping minds of others to influence them? You were handed that technique and told precisely what to say and do. Use that method for all you're worth!

Simultaneously, refine your own personality and image with the *Third* and *Eleventh Secrets*, adding the *Fourteenth* if necessary.

Then, when you're in the physical presence of the object of your desire, or someone you believe may become your partner soon, use the *Tenth Secret: The Stupendous Power Enricher*.

Recall how you envisaged a powerful jet of steam rushing from between your eyes to form a cloud around whatever is in front of you?

When you're in front of your partner target, pretend that is exactly what is happening. The "steam" (which is really a cloud of Cosmic Energy) is enveloping the person. No need to close your eyes or do anything unusual: just recall the exercise you went through in the privacy of your *Secret* practice; you did all the work before, so *Confidential Corporeal Commands* are also unneeded at this confrontation time.

Just one application of the Energy cloud will suffice, when the two of you are in conversation.

Take advantage of the charming results.

AGE OR APPEARANCE IS UNIMPORTANT

Despite the way advertising and society lay emphasis on youth and beauty these days, *New Avatar Power* easily enables you to hurdle such imaginary barriers.

No matter if you think you're too old, unattractive, under privileged, or handicapped in the game of love, *New Avatar Power* immerses you in a powerful aura of attraction, and your partners will see you in a different light. What you may have thought were personal drawbacks to attracting a mate will turn out to be your greatest and unique assets.

AN ARCANE TRUTH ABOUT MARRIAGE BONDS

One thing I must soberly advise you. If you try to use *New Avatar Power* to steal someone else's legal spouse, you're up against a powerful *Magical Ritual*, unless *both* parties to the marriage have agreed to end it.

The marriage ceremony, whether a full-scale white wedding in a church or performed by a registrar is backed by *Unseen Magic* predating *New Avatar Power* and most other psychic and occult methods known today.

The knot which is tied between man and wife is more powerful than almost all other magic. So here we run into the one area where *New Avatar Power* meets its match. Recall that in your love relationships and you'll suffer fewer disappointments.

THE CHOICE IS YOURS

Magnetism or coercion? Are you going to set yourself up as a radiator of love vibrations or actively manipulate your desired partner by *Astral Travel* and *Dream Manipulation*?

If you're in a hurry to get a partner and have a suitable compatible person in mind, coercion, invisible and powerful, is your method.

Alternatively, if you'd like to savor the surprise of having destiny bring your perfect love to you, maybe someone you've never even thought about, never even met becoming a love magnet, is best.

Either way, fulfillment is close. Open up with the *Exceptional Love Elevator* and find perfect harmony.

SUMMARY OF CHAPTER 9

1. You deserve the right partner. *New Avatar Power* will work that miracle for you.
2. *New Avatar Power* is in its natural element when influencing emotional and romantic conditions.
3. The *Exceptional Love Elevator* works on bringing a known or unknown partner to you, or will turn an existing relationship into everything you desire.
4. Reinforce *New Avatar Power's* unseen work with activities intentionally putting you in line for love satisfaction.
5. *New Avatar Power* turns what you may think are personal disadvantages into unique love assets.
6. You're up against powerful Magic if you try to break up an existing marriage.
7. Choose either or both, magnetism or coercion, to find perfect love.

Secrets of Good Fortune Through Amazing New Avatar Power

10

SECRETS OF GOOD FORTUNE THROUGH AMAZING NEW AVATAR POWER

Everyone seeks good luck, and all too few find it in regular doses. Here we're looking at *New Avatar Power* ways of doing just that: bringing bounty to you by wooing Lady Luck, charming Dame Fortune, or manipulating coincidence to put you ahead of less lucky colleagues.

SECRETS OF GOOD FORTUNE

WHAT'S YOUR IDEA OF GOOD LUCK?

A primary definition will aid you in setting up your *Luck Targets*. What's your idea of "being lucky"? Regular wins with lottery tickets? Beating the tables at Reno? Gaining respect and kudos by being noticed? Finding perfect living conditions? Solving problems quickly by sparkling hunches?

Any, all, or none of the above can be your idea of "luck" in the broad sense. But if you see luck merely as being able to win a contest whenever you please, the foregoing may have opened your eyes a trifle.

Yes, *New Avatar Power* will improve your luck, whatever you're involved in. But when it comes down to the crunch, anticipating being the *one* person whose ticket is drawn from ten million or so, you're doing some very precise focusing, and when I say *New Avatar Power* automatically chooses the most harmonious path, I mean it. So being a feted and famous millionaire from winning a lottery may *not* be *New Avatar Power's* way of bringing you to total happiness, so your dollars laid out on lottery tickets can be money in someone else's pocket.

I mention this at the beginning to be totally frank with you. I know many people who have used *New Avatar Power* and promptly bought the winning ticket, or beaten the bank at Lake Tahoe. It works, and the *Marvelous Luck Changer* is certain to change your luck.

But improving your luck may be different from your expectations. I have a letter from one disgruntled gambler who said he agreed *New Avatar Power* improved his luck, but he was still unsatisfied. Previously, most of his selections at the track had run no place, still slogging away long after the winner was past the post.

After using *New Avatar Power* his selections were doing a great deal better. His horses were coming in second, third, sometimes fourth. Occasionally he was finding winners. But overall, although his luck had *improved*, he was even more frustrated because he was coming *closer* to the money, but still not winning much.

I suggested *New Avatar Power* was not only working for him, it was also trying to tell him something: try your luck in some other area. He took the hint, and now he's a plutocrat, having used his talents in investment counseling.

VcToria Comments: I also believe that using this type of magic for horse racing is archaic. When you use animals in any shape, form or otherwise, it is abuse. Animals did not come into this world to be used for money gain. That you will understand as enlightenment shapes your life.

So the word is, *New Avatar Power* will change your luck, but you may have to seek out the *area* which it's operating in. For reasons spelled out below, winning lotteries, bingo, craps, horses, dogs, numbers, and the like may not be your most harmonious path to contentment.

HOW LUCK WORKS

You've come across the expression "lucky streak," meaning a time when no matter what chance you take you win. Some people seem to have their lucky streaks more often than others, while some say they *never* have a lucky break.

Luck undeniably comes in spasms, in regular swings. People who seem to be constantly lucky are those who, by instinct or deliberate life arrangement, are catching their luck cycles at their peaks and cashing in.

The losers of this world *do* have their lucky times, but some inner drive makes them take chances when their luck tides are at low ebb, so they lose much more often than they win.

Astrologers know these cycles well, and many people have used the swings of their horoscopes to win.

VcToria Comments: As I have mentioned in previous books, I do offer *Lucky Gambling Charts* on my web store that correlate to your astrological planetary placements. I do not guarantee a 100% win for you, but will place you at the best time to buy or bet. You will also get numbers that correspond to you personally.

What *New Avatar Power* will do for you is to break your cycle of bad luck, which has you taking chances at the wrong times, and place you in a routine where you take chances at the *right* times. Then you're aligned for maximum opportunities to win in the battle of life.

HOW TO HELP LADY LUCK SMILE ON YOU

The answer to getting lucky is simple. You take chances when the swings of fate are in your favor and swinging away from your opponents. When the reverse happens, and others are getting lucky, you lie low and do nothing.

Knowing *when* to do this is the challenge. That's where the *Marvelous Luck Changer* comes into its own.

TWENTIETH SECRET OF NEW AVATAR POWER: THE MARVELOUS LUCK CHANGER

"I *never* get lucky. Not once in my whole life have I ever been lucky." If that's your cry, I'd strongly advise you to back off from taking any kinds of chances until

SECRETS OF GOOD FORTUNE

you've changed your mind. *Everyone* has tides of luck. What you're saying is that you've never taken a chance at a time when your luck patterns were running good. That's another story.

A colleague of mine who calls herself *Undine,* and studies numerology, gets many letters from people who say they're in deep money trouble, and they're battling to get out by playing the numbers, so can she give them some numbers which will win for them?

Undine almost always tries to get one point across to her correspondent. If he or she is in money trouble, his luck must be in a bad swing. So no amount of gambling will locate good luck. Such people should wait until their luck swings positive, and *then* try.

Unfortunately a myth has crept into popular use that, no matter when or where, some magical person can hand out a bunch of numbers which are unerringly "lucky." It's not so. If you're into a swing of "bad" luck you can gamble on every number from one to infinity, and you'll pick the wrong ones, and win nothing more than a cold.

Yes, you can change "bad" luck to "better" luck (like my frustrated gambler correspondent whose selections finished further up the field but still out of the money), but you have to keep in mind the Shakespearean truth that

> There is a tide in the affairs of men,
> Which, taken at the flood, leads on to fortune.

This *Twentieth Secret* enables you to catch that tide when it's in full flood and lead yourself to your desired fortune.

Build this routine into your *New Avatar Power* work, about once a month. Recite your *Confidential Corporeal Commands* and plant your usual board or screen.

SECRETS OF GOOD FORTUNE

Imagine you're writing on the board, or someone is writing it for you, the number 3332. That is the *Number of Luck*.

Note: I have *not* said that's a Lucky Number, so trying to buy tickets with that number on them is leaping off at the wrong tangent.

Think about that number. Say it to yourself: "Three-three-three-two." Familiarize yourself with it, so you can recall it at any time. It's a simple one to recall, but it makes powerful metaphysical connections between you and your world of chance.

You now have at your command the most potent key known to connect your conscious thinking patterns with your unseen luck tides.

Open your eyes, and go about your business. But recall that number and regularly reconnect your inner being with it.

HOW TO USE THE MARVELOUS LUCK CHANGER

Like many other aspects of *New Avatar Power*, you use the *Marvelous Luck Changer* in combination with other *Secrets* and techniques.

The *Marvelous Luck Changer*, once you've set the inner wheels in motion, ensures that any other *Secret* you use it with directs you toward luck and the consequences of whatever you, personally, see as "being lucky."

In effect you "place" the *Number of Luck* in your mind and being, then "call" on its powers whenever you need them.

If any element of luck or chance is involved in your desired outcome of any *Secret*, as you open your eyes at the end, say the *Number of Luck* once to yourself.

With the *Number of Luck* placed into life's situations, you're aligned with whatever "lucky breaks" are

SECRETS OF GOOD FORTUNE

around, and if you follow your hunches, you'll be in the right place at the right time, you'll know *when* to gamble, and when to stay away from lotteries, numbers, or any other games of chance.

DISCOVERING WINNING NUMBERS

I trust you have read, understood, and considered the earlier part of this chapter. I know the temptation to extract this piece from the rest of the book and try to build a new life on it. I'll say it again: dipping into and taking bits which you fancy from this book is futile: it not only means I've wasted my time in writing 65,000 words, it also means the chances are you'll be disappointed.

Yes, you can discover Winning Numbers this way. But please do not make them the sole solution to life's problems: if fate has you in a corner, it's going to take more than lucky numbers to battle your way free.

To discover Winning Numbers first set up the conditions for them to be selected. If it's a lottery, how many numbers occur on each ticket—is it a five-figure number, six-figure, or how many? If you're going to Reno to try roulette, your limits of numbers are 1 through 36, of course, but recall zero and double-zero: they're in the chance pattern too.

Having set up the picture in your mind, with the sort of numbers you're looking for, perform the *Magic Future Knowing Technique* as explained in Chapter 6.

Before you pretend the calendar pages are drifting off, think "Three-three-three-two, in a kind of loud, mental statement. Pretend you're saying it to a crowd of people in a fair-sized room, so they'll all hear it. But do not speak it aloud.

Then proceed with the *Magic Future Knowing Technique* as I explained previously.

177

SECRETS OF GOOD FORTUNE

When you wake, instead of grabbing the story told by your dreams, latch onto any numbers your inner mind showed in the sleep state. You'll find they fit to the proposal you were considering when you began the *Secret*. Write those numbers down before they slip away.

They will win for you, and *New Avatar Power* builds in a purposeful fail-safe mechanism. If you do *not* dream anything which fits to your Lucky Numbers proposal of the preceding night, that's a clear signal you're into a swing of luck where winning is unlikely. Prompted by the magic *Number of Luck*, your *New Avatar Power* will assuredly hand you what you need to win *when the time is right*.

It's simple, foolproof, and automatic, geared to your *personal* luck patterns by the all-knowing insight of *New Avatar Power*.

SUMMARY OF CHAPTER 10

1. Yes, *New Avatar Power* can change your luck.
2. Set up *Luck Targets*.
3. Improving your luck may bring different results from your expectations.
4. Everyone's luck swings up and down regularly. Astrologers know these cycles. There are no guarantees but VcToria does offer a Lucky Gambling Chart on her web store.
5. *New Avatar Power* will break your cycle of bad luck.
6. If you're into a "bad luck" cycle, you're very unlikely to win.
7. *New Avatar Power* will automatically identify the right *times* when you can gamble with reasonable prospects of success.
8. The *Number of Luck* stirs your inner mind and puts you in the right place at the right time.

9. Selecting winning numbers in your sleep is simple, because *New Avatar Power* will wait until your luck is in a positive swing for you. It's so easy, you literally do it with your eyes closed.

Secrets of Escaping From Domination Using New Avatar Power

11

SECRETS OF ESCAPING FROM DOMINATION USING NEW AVATAR POWER

What's holding you back from the epitome of harmony which you deserve? This chapter can give you new insight into unseen obstacles to personal progress and enable you to pull yourself free.

HOW TO RECOGNIZE THE DOMINATION WHICH IS CRIPPLING YOU

We're all subject to obeying laws, from Natural Law which operates throughout the Universe, down to

ESCAPING FROM DOMINATION

manmade laws which help society to run as smoothly as possible.

Those are inescapable, and if you object to a law, the harmonious thing to do is to get it changed. Flouting any law is hazardous, although trying to oppose Natural Law is the most dangerous of all.

What do I mean by that last? Again, a material example. A Natural Law, which is usefully employed inside your automobile, says that when gasoline is ignited, it burns or explodes. Trying to oppose that Natural Law hurts. If you pour gasoline over your clothing, and apply a lighted match, you'll *burn*. No amount of insisting "I believe this Natural Law to be unfair, restrictive, and unconstitutional" will keep you out of a hospital bed.

That's a very obvious attempt to oppose Natural Law which is so well-known and evident that we recognize it easily. Other Natural Laws are less obvious, but opposing them can be almost as hurtful.

So we're under domination like that, and *New Avatar Power* aids you in harmonizing with such Laws, instead of fighting them. *New Avatar Power* will also help you overcome other restrictions which form the subject of this chapter. These restrictions are domination which comes from someone or something, backed by neither manmade nor Natural Laws.

First you have to recognize such domination, and it can be subtle in the extreme. The wife who becomes sick when her spouse wants to go to the ballgame is dominating her man by emotional means. The mother who says she'll do away with herself if her son marries his choice of girlfriend is another blatant example.

Your boss who wields the threat of dismissal over you if you step out of line is also dominating.

Even closer to home, your own fears of "What if it failed to work out right" can dominate your freedom to grow toward the happiness you seek.

So if life is changing too slowly for your liking, if so far the application of *New Avatar Power* has resulted in fewer changes than you had anticipated, wonder if the chains of domination are what are holding you back.

ESCAPING FROM DOMINATION

First identify the source of the domination. Then build a shield against it. Spend a few minutes considering what is frustrating you, what's standing in your way of achieving your goals, who wields power over you which is neither from manmade laws nor from Natural Law.

Your *Mystical Initiation* list will help you identify the domination. From that list you should be able to clearly see where more work needs to be done to free yourself.

If it's a self-generated fear which is holding you back, you already have the tool to solve that. Apply the *Fabulous Fear Eradicator* as directed in Chapter Two.

Does your domination come from one or more of the *Seven Negative Traps?* No. 6: *Over-Sensitivity to the Influence of Others* often holds worthy people back from achievement. And No. 7: *Too Involved with the Troubles of Others* is a special obstacle which takes careful solving, simply because we're taught, correctly, that compassion for the unfortunate is desirable. So it is, but reread that section of Chapter 5 to realize when compassion can go too far.

Having identified the source of the domination which is holding you back, be it a person or circumstance, apply the *Wonderful Over-Concern Protector*. It's purposely and purposefully designed to eliminate such opposition to your right to be happy and free.

ESCAPING FROM DOMINATION

TWENTY-FIRST SECRET OF NEW AVATAR POWER: THE WONDERFUL OVER-CONCERN PROTECTOR

The final *Secret* herewith, the most useful and powerful of all. If I had to select but one *Secret* from all twenty-one, this is the one I would master. First, because it's ultimately powerful, and second because it uses several preceding *Secrets*!

Carry out the *Sixteenth Secret*, then sit or lie down and mentally position your usual screen or board.

Pretend this time you're in front of a mirror. Naturally, you'll see yourself reflected in it. Consider who or what is dominating you, and as you run the thoughts through your mind, sketch in the idea that the "you" in the mirror is tightly bound with chains.

By the time you've considered your domination sources fully, your pretend reflection should look like Houdini about to do his famous escape from enough chains to sink a battleship.

In your mind, state the *Number of Luck*. You're going to need luck as well as planning if your domination is as forceful and subtle as most people's.

Erase the picture in the mirror in your usual way. Now fish around in your memory for a time when you were freed from some restriction. Put a picture on your screen of your running happily home from school after class; a mental picture of your running away from home, being released from jail, getting away from employment you disliked. It has to be some personal situation which you've experienced and can recall with reasonable clarity.

Having acted that little cameo through in your memory, carry out the *Incredible Disinterest Remover*. No need to include the *Confidential Corporeal Commands*, nor are they needed for the last step in this

Secret: perform the *Phenomenal Over-Sensitivity Transformer.*

Are you ever charged up to work miracles now! That combination of internal mind work throws *New Avatar Power* into fast four-wheel drive. Nothing can stand in your way for long now.

DEFEATING YOUR ENEMIES

Protecting yourself from all manner of negativity is the purpose of the *Wonderful Over-Concern Protector.* With the addition of the *Stupendous Power Enricher* you can almost literally blow away your oppositions.

When you know an enemy is working against you, carry out those two *Secrets*, in the order mentioned. When you come to the "steam projection" device, pretend it's gushing all over your enemy, shriveling him or her (or them), bowling them over and crushing them to the ground.

If you happen to *meet* a known enemy face to face at any time within 14 days of carrying out the *Wonderful Over-Concern Protector* you can get even deeper into your enemy's being. With your eyes open, so no one thinks you're up to anything strange, pretend you're performing the *Stupendous Power Enricher* "blowing away" technique.

REMOVING CURSES, THE EVIL EYE OR POSSESSION

Really and truly, powerful curses and the "Evil Eye" are rare commodities in this day and age. The techniques and abilities take much work and energy. Frankly, most of the people who have reputations for doing evil by occult means rely on fear, imagination, myths, and legends to do their unpleasant work for them.

ESCAPING FROM DOMINATION

Nevertheless, it's just possible you may be under domination from someone who knows the *Old Ways* and is a practitioner of *Black* or *Gray Magic.*

If so, you're now protected, if you've followed with me through the *Secrets of New Avatar Power.* And you now own the ultimate weapon to throw the evil back to its source. *New Avatar Power* inserts a neat check and balance here: when you apply the following technique, evil magic is hurled back to its source and the sender receives the effects she or he was projecting. Results are almost instantaneous: the evil-sender will suffer harm of some kind or another within hours.

Here's the safety-valve: if the target of the returned evil is either innocent or is merely playing on your fears and emotions, *nothing will happen.* Yes, *New Avatar Power* will unerringly reflect evil magic back to its source with devastating efficiency.

But if the evil emanation does not exist, you'll see very little happen to the alleged malefactor. So you'll have to seek further to find out why you consider you're bewitched.

That's the splendid feature of this *Secret*: if you happen to be mistaken, you cannot do damage to innocent parties. If you're correct, the malefactor is smashed.

So if you really and genuinely feel you're under magical domination, or you're having the Evil Eye cast at you, perform the *Twenty-First Secret* when the Moon is new.

As you end the *Secret,* add one extra detail. Pretend for about a minute that your box of clear bullet-proof glass is also *silvered,* so you're looking at the backs of reflecting mirrors surrounding you. Thus any streams of energy directed at you at occult levels are reflected back with shattering force to wherever they're coming from.

ESCAPING FROM DOMINATION

That's all. Listen for news of your Evil Eye practitioner. If indeed the negative aspect of the occult is being practiced against you, or any other variation of evil Magic, you'll see the devastating results visited upon your attacker within hours.

SUMMARY OF CHAPTER 11

1. Recognize who or what is dominating you.
2. Harmonize with *Natural Law* and find happiness and freedom.
3. Use the *Wonderful Over-Concern Protector* to eliminate domination.
4. "Blow away" your enemies with the *Stupendous Power Enricher*.
5. True occult curses are fairly rare these days.
6. If you are under a spell, affected by the Evil Eye, cursed or possessed by demons, adding the deflecting mirror technique to the *Twenty First Secret* will blast the evil-doer.
7. No harm will come to anyone if you should happen to be mistaken about the source of the evil which comes your way. The innocent will not be harmed.

Creating Your Perfect Life With New Avatar Power

12

CREATING YOUR PERFECT LIFE WITH NEW AVATAR POWER

Twenty-one secrets and a host of tips and wrinkles have been laid before you, enabling you to employ the awesome energy of the Cosmos, which I have called *New Avatar Power*. The paths of your mind and body are opening up, making a broad superhighway for *New Avatar Power* to sweep in and obey your smallest wish, clearing away frustrations, fears, and obstacles, leading you to the peace, harmony, and luxury you entertained only as hopeful dreams before. Those dreams are now about to become total and true reality.

BEST WAYS TO APPLY THE WHOLE NEW AVATAR POWER TECHNIQUE

Sooner or later, someone is going to say to you: "*New Avatar Power* is false: it pretends it can give you something for nothing, and everyone knows you *can't* get something for nothing."

That statement is untrue. I lived in a house in Muldersdrift, South Africa, which used solar panels for all heating and hot water. Once the basic work was done, the Sun provided us with copious energy which didn't cost us a thin dime. You're using *New Avatar Power* in the same way. Just as solar energy is free, so Cosmic Energy is free, and once you've built yourself into an efficient receiver of the energy by applying the *Secrets*, so you *do* get things for nothing: Cosmic Energy does the work.

But concerning such negative reactions to your use of *New Avatar Power,* attracting such attention is undesirable. So in order to avoid the gloom-and-doom brigade who will try to put you down, keep your use of *New Avatar Power* a personal secret. You'll get results quicker if you're not surrounded by unbelievers.

Set up your *New Avatar Power* program. Identify your problems, decide what you wish to have replace them, and apply the *Secrets* to work the miracles.

DETAILS TO WATCH

I've done my very best to lay out this program so that you can tailor it easily to transforming your life.

Inevitably, questions will arise. For instance, if you're working more than one *Secret* at a sitting, is it necessary to start each *Secret* with the *Confidential*

Corporeal Commands? Answer: No. Once you have recited your *Commands*, you can follow them with any number of *Secrets*.

Maybe you have trouble deciding if you're lonely, in despair, or merely unhappy. Which *Secret* should you apply? Answer: apply all three appropriate ones to cancel the condition. No one ever came to harm from an overdose of *New Avatar Power*: no such thing exists as *too much* Cosmic Energy usage.

The one minor caution I insert is that you balance your use of *New Avatar Power* with your regular duties, obligations, and responsibilities. *New Avatar Power* must *not* interfere with day-to-day routines. For example, it's invalid to turn up late for work saying, "Sorry I'm late, my *New Avatar Power* work took me longer than I expected."

No doubt you'll have your own queries and points of doubt about how, where, and when to apply *New Avatar Power*.

Best course is to solve the questions *in your own way*. The whole of this course of using *New Avatar Power* is geared to your way of doing things, your way of thinking, your psychology. The whole program you work out is individual: no one in the whole wide world will apply *New Avatar Power* in exactly the way you do.

I have given you the ground rules: you apply them in any way you think fit, and *for you*, those ways will be the best ways, because they fit like a glove to your mind, having been produced by your mind.

As I said early on, do not get hung up on details. You'll pay attention to the *New Avatar Power* activities, of course. Rushing a *Secret*, or getting sloppy with your *New Avatar Work* will produce sloppy results. But on the other hand, relaxed and peaceful use of *Cosmic Energy* is your aim at all times.

CREATING YOUR PERFECT LIFE

FOLLOW THE INSTRUCTIONS AND YOUR MIRACLES ARRIVE

In a book such as this, you need to extract what applies to you and pass over that which is not relevant to your life style and conditions.

Secrets 1, 4, and 8, plus the *Confidential Corporeal Commands* and *Mystic Initiation* are universal to all users of this method. The other *Secrets* you select, use as and when you wish to apply them.

But I strongly advise you work through this book from cover to cover, practicing the techniques so they come easily to mind as you use them. Even if a *Secret* does not apply right now, doing a dry run with it is valuable *New Avatar Power* practice.

DAILY NEW AVATAR POWER WORKOUT IS BEST

Set up your *New Avatar Program* to fit into your daily routines. If possible, a few minutes in the quiet each day should be your aim, with a slightly longer session on a monthly basis, to "boost" various *Secrets* as I've explained.

Of course, the *Mysterious N'T Word Game* can be played whenever you think of it, while your *Confidential Corporeal Commands* are valuable for detaching from tense situations, as I pointed out earlier.

New Avatar Power becomes a part of your life eventually. You live with its in-pouring, knowing that even when you're immersed in the most mundane task, *New Avatar Power* is helping things along, quietly shaping your future into the glory you aspire to.

TOTAL ATTUNEMENT USING NEW AVATAR POWER

Knitting everything which has gone before into a coherent package for you. Here is a summary of your personal *New Avatar Power* program.

1. See and hear Cosmic Energy. Required one time only, but repeat if you feel the need.
2. Understand and remember the *First Secret*.
3. Decide what needs changing with the help of your *Mystic Initiation*.
4. List what's wrong with your life, and number the problems in priority order. Also make a list of suitable solutions. These lists should be rearranged monthly.
5. Create your *Confidential Corporeal Commands*. Recite them in all tension situations.
6. Establish (as feasible) a daily time to recite your *Confidential Corporeal Commands*. As you learn other *Secrets*, this time becomes your *New Avatar Power* working period each day (except for the techniques which are used at bedtime).
7. Clear your *New Avatar Power* channel by playing the *Mysterious N'T Word Game* whenever you please.
8. Create your *Personal Verbal Seals*.
9. Make a record of life conditions, create your *Mental Achievement Chalkboard*, and write your *Total Happiness List*, revising each of these monthly.
10. Practice *Charging Your Aura With Cosmic Energy* when required.
11. Escape from domination with the *Twenty-First Secret*.
12. Apply *Secrets 5, 6, 7, and 9 through 20* as and when necessary, using them in the suggested ways, and following up on any revelations which bring any goal closer.

CREATING YOUR PERFECT LIFE

Once you've tested out each of the *Secrets*, you begin to be selective. Each time you sit or lie down to work with *New Avatar Power* techniques, decide on what miracle, or miracles you'll aim at this day.

For example, you might select a solution from your *Mystic Initiation* list, and bring it to you as explained. Then proceed to eradicate a fear, improve your health, and polish your luck a bit. These are your selections, depending on what needs doing most and how much time you've allocated for this *New Avatar Power* routine. But please do not rush and hurry too much: one miracle fully achieved is better than ten miracles only partly accomplished!

And of course, if you feel you just have too many goals and have trouble selecting a few for the day, use the *Fifth Secret* to make your decisions for you.

There you have your program. Personally tailored to bring your every desire into glittering, fulfilling reality. Go to it, and may you realize every wish which you've ever wished—plus a few more that *New Avatar Power* has in store for you, better, more stupendous, and more amazing than anything you thought possible.

Epilog: Some Personal Thoughts To You From The Author In 1978

Geof Gray-Cobb
August 15th 1928-Deceased May 12th 2009

EPILOG: SOME PERSONAL THOUGHTS TO YOU FROM THE AUTHOR IN 1978

Geof Gray-Cobb
August 15th 1928-Deceased May 12th 2009

Four years ago I wrote a book called *The Miracle of New Avatar Power*. Reader response was fantastic, awesome. Letters flooded in, and even as I read the first of your myriad responses, I realized here was a mother lode of first-hand experience which could be mined to the benefit of all.

Into my mail box was pouring a golden treasury of data from the very people I had set out to reach.

EPILOG

People without whom an author is merely a typist: his readers, bless you all!

Within those envelopes sent to me from the far corners of this earth I found questions, comments, constructive criticism and friendly dialogs. From those grew this book. Better and easier to use. Techniques which confused people have been smoothed and clarified. Emphasis has been placed on factors I previously failed to point up adequately enough.

And you will realize I was able to do this only with help. Your help.

Many of you out there can feel a glow of pleasure as you realize you aided me in my task of making *New Avatar Power* more beneficial, more universal in effect. A few of you will be able to show your friends the case histories. "That's me he's writing about—and it's all true," you'll say. Others will recognize how I've changed parts of the *New Avatar Power* method to circumvent difficulties they wrote to me about.

Yes, I read all incoming mail personally: the fact that *your* letter does not appear in this book is merely a witness to the sheer volume of mail which arrived—I had to be very selective.

Indeed, this has been a two-way street. I put the words together the best I know how, and you told me where I was right, where I went wrong, where I should have expressed myself more plainly. And as an author must if he is to grow, I've used your feedback to provide significant substance in these pages—and I will use more in the pages of other books to come.

As you will have realized, my purpose in writing books such as this one is to help you help yourself. And I can best do that if I know your problems, share your successes, am aware of your failures, so that I may try my best to straighten out the way ahead for you with my writings.

EPILOG

I know reader response will be as voluminous and gratifying as it was for my first book. I just hope you understand that it is virtually impossible for me to reply to each and every letter I receive. But know that I have read your letter, and shared your joys or sorrows.

I'm deeply interested in how you're getting along with *New Avatar Power*. Maybe in a later book, you'll see clear evidence of that, as I respond to your comments, and you'll feel the warm pleasure of recognizing how you have been instrumental in helping others to greater happiness and harmony.

A simple "Thank you for your trouble, time and stamps," is the best I can do. Keep those letters flowing in, my friends: without them I have no way of knowing if I'm hitting the right targets for you.

NEW AVATAR POWER IS WAITING TO SERVE YOU

My labor of love is virtually complete. Here you have my latest thoughts and techniques on using *New Avatar Power* to transform your life, to bring your every last dream into glittering fulfillment.

This method has developed directly from the original method, written up in my previous book, *The Miracle of New Avatar Power*. Readers of that book will recognize the streamlining, the logical flow of techniques, to make the process even more automatic, even more powerful and fantastic.

"Should I use the original method, or this new one?" is an inevitable closing query for some. My answer is: "If the original method is working well for you and you have your *Cosmic Chart* clicking into place, stay with it. If you feel you'd like to incorporate this method, your *Magic Mentor* will show you how."

And if that preceding paragraph puzzles you, know that it concerned a part of *New Avatar Power* which I included in my previous book. No need to

EPILOG

worry: in a different form, it's part of this new book, so you're not being deprived of anything. Only the *Names* have been changed to protect the confused!

Be peaceful, work with the *Secrets*, and when we meet in the Astral Plane, we shall salute each other.
May all your miracles be vouchsafed you.

Epilog from VcToria: Thank You all for keeping my late Fathers work alive. Having been inundated with requests to republish his works of the mid seventies to early eighties, I have now done so. I did release them in an order I felt comfortable with. See the index.

Today letters are not the normal way of correspondence. I am fine with this, as I have kept up with technology as it unfolded. You now have a Face Book page dedicated to comments and discussions on all of his books. I welcome all who wish to join, and welcome all comments there:
www.facebook.com/GeofGrayCobb

In the slightly re-edited books that I now have republished, I have removed most, if not all, of the testimonials. If you still wish to read those, you can purchase an original book on Amazon for a lot less in cost than what they were in previous years prior to my new publications.

All five of Dad's books have now been republished. I do recommend buying all of them, either for the wonderful changes they will produce and/or for the collector's items that they one day will be again.

In 2020 I will be publishing an amazing book. I am taking all of Dad's five books, and choosing the best of the best magic to shift your life. PLUS not only that, my mother wrote two books on Angels, and I will be

EPILOG

taking the best of the best from those two and adding in your Angel magic. PLUS, adding my own magic to shift and guide you.

Many have asked about the 26 page booklet that dad wrote on Astral travelling. I will be adding that to the *Encyclopedia of 50 Year Old* Magic with your Guides/Angels and Magic Mentors as I plan to call it.

Please know that I wrote my own 'memoir' in 2017 that takes the reader through a life of craziness. At the age of 21 I fell in love with a bank robber. This shifted my life, but not only that, it brought me to the brink of 'how or who am I'? I had to choose to 'sink or swim'. Only because of my cats, did I choose to 'swim'.

I thank the Universe for all the golden rainbows that were gifted to me in the shape of magic, luck, synchronicities, and so much more while I 'swam'. To my cats, Lucas, Sammy and Princess thank you. If it were not for you I would not have 'escaped' the addictions I created with my lack of knowing what life was all about.

To understand that all I write about is 100% of what I went through you may buy the memoir on my website or through Amazon. Please buy the 'updated' book as this answers the cliff hanging chapter of the first book. *Then Now and Forever* by VcToria Gray-Cobb. [Updated book]

The first book is written and titled the same, but by VcToria Gray.

Again, the immense gratitude I feel towards all of the folks who still support my Dad's work, is truly heartfelt. I meditate for you all under the Pisces Moon once a month. As I have stated many times in the previous books, you may join me in the comfort of your own home. I post the times on the Face Book page. In *The Mystic Grimoire of Mighty Spells and Rituals* by Frater Malak [aka Geof Gray-Cobb] and *NAP* by Geof Gray-Cobb [this being his follow up book] there is a 'spell', or

EPILOG

as I like to call it, an invitation of energy to bring the astral plane of Dad's soul energy to join us, and send your requests to the correct area of working. See the last pages in both re-published books.

                    Positive Thoughts To You All,
                    VcToria Gray-Cobb.

CPSIA information can be obtained
at www.ICGtesting.com
Printed in the USA
LVHW011925050221
678444LV00002B/164

9 781999 128326